With God My Helper

With God My Helper

Ruth Sanford

Marshalls

First published by Servant Books, P.O. Box 8617, Ann Arbor, Michigan 48107 1981

First published in the UK 1982 by Marshall Morgan & Scott, 1 Bath Street, London, EC1V 9LB

Where portions of the scripture quotations appear in italics, the emphasis has been added by the author.

ISBN: 0 551 00965 9

Printed in England by Hunt Barnard Printing

Contents

Introduction

When I was very young the drawing room of my great aunt's house always seemed small and dark to me, with drab colors and drawn curtains. Whenever we visited her, we ended up in that room, where I felt so much like a prisoner. The conversation was about people I didn't know, places I had never been, and issues beyond my comprehension. Although I liked my great aunt and uncle, I would eagerly await my release to the outside, where I could run around to explore the yard.

One particular day we had just settled in the drawing room for a visit when I noticed a small lamp on a drop-leaf table. It was hung round about with ten prisms, which I discovered could be easily removed. As I took one off to get a closer look, it passed by a crack in the curtains. Suddenly I was staring at a rainbow, made all the more brilliant by the darkness that had preceded it. I had never seen anything quite so exquisite in its simplicity. How could something so plain one minute look so lovely the next?

I looked up to show the prism to my mother and saw the same brilliance reflected on the wall. The drawing room was suddenly transformed from a dark, dreary room to a place of delight. From then on I was allowed to place the lamp in the window, moving the prisms to catch the light.

After that, I no longer spent my time wishing I was outside. I began to enjoy listening to the conversation, and even to anticipate future visits with eagerness. The drawing room had been transformed from a dark prison to a place of beauty and of happy fellowship.

All too often we view our own lives exactly as I used to view my great aunt's drawing room—as dark and boring prisons. Yet every life has the potential to be beautiful and delightful. The drawing room is made up of the circumstances of our lives that cannot easily change—our home, family, job, and economic situation. We are the lamps, stable fixtures in the room. The prisms are the qualities of our personalities and attributes of our characters. Each of us has great potential because every set of curtains can open enough for the light of God to shine through.

But often our prisms are hanging plain and dusty, unable to reflect the light. We need to allow them to be dusted, polished, and held up to the light. Only then can we delight in their brilliance. Our lives will be filled with the joy and peace that God intends, because we will reflect his glory.

You may wonder what all of this has to do with real life. How is it going to get you through the next day, the next time your four-year-old whines, your teenager sulks, your ten-year-old swears, the supper burns, the baby acts collicky, your husband cannot find clean socks, the washer overflows, the drains clog, and your six-year-old walks up with a half-eaten apple to say that he found a dismembered worm inside?

Any woman with a family knows that all these things could happen tomorrow. Perhaps your first response is to picture yourself leaving a note on the refrigerator (next to everyone else's), calling the nearest Holiday Inn for a room near the pool, and deciding to stay there until somebody calls to say they've got the house and children in order, and it's OK for you to return.

Then reason raises its head and you brush this idea aside. You might start asking God to do something, hoping that, just this once, he will send his angels to restore you, repair the appliances, and hand out peaceful spirits to everyone, like so many tranquilizers. Eventually, though, you've got to face the inevitable. It's up to you to right the relationships, call the plumber, clean up the spills, calm the baby, fold the laundry, discipline the children, cook the supper, and maintain order. It's no wonder that the prisms are hanging dusty and unchanged by the light if you're still trying to catch up with last week, let alone taking time to let "his Spirit make you to be strong in your inner selves" (Eph 3:16).

Perhaps your days are much more ordered than that. You may have one, two, several, or no children. You may work outside the home and have an orderly well-established routine. Yet you may still feel that you lack something. Anxiety may attack you even when things are working quite smoothly. Perhaps you always seem to owe someone a letter, need to clean a cupboard, or finish your current refurbishing project.

Some of us are not consciously bothered by the work. We've perfected techniques for avoiding it. We lead busy lives that block out all the troublesome areas. Or we may have no problem completing our work but become frustrated and bored when we haven't enough to do.

What most of us have in common is that we can't seem to be simply at rest and at peace, to relax and enjoy ourselves, our husbands, and our children. It's difficult to experience the fullness of God's love surrounding us. We find it hard to let go of our burdens, the worries and anxieties that float in and out of our consciousness. We all see areas in our relationships with others that need improvement, and we may be discontented with life as we are presently leading it.

Now if I claimed that I have overcome every difficulty with ease and that I always felt wonderful, my nose would grow longer than Pinocchio's. I have had very good days and very bad ones, as have most of us. But I have learned to be more than a survivor. Instead of feeling pulled in fifteen different directions at once, I have learned that Jesus does have a plan to keep me in one piece and at peace. I have learned to be content as I go through my days, dealing with crises as they come up.

Through sharing with other women, some with similar family situations and some with very different ones, I have learned that there are practical things to do each day that will win us victories in Jesus' name. We can grow in strength, compassion, patience, endurance, joy, trust, faith, hope, and even love while in the midst of situations that might otherwise make us callous and bitter. We are lamps hung round about with prisms, placed in the drawing rooms of our lives. In most cases the lamps will stay within the same room. The choice is ours whether to allow our prisms to hang dusty and lifeless or to let them glow with a myriad of color and light.

I hope that what is offered in the pages that follow will help you to blow off the dust and polish the glass of your lamp, that you may reflect the glory of God. Once you choose life you can be assured that victory is yours through the power of the Holy Spirit.

Part I

Overcoming Personal Difficulties

God has a glorious plan for women in his kingdom—one that includes a way of life that is rich, varied, exciting, and fulfilling. This was his plan from the beginning. And Jesus' life, death, and resurrection have made it possible.

Many women believe this but don't know how to make this truth a reality in their lives. Indeed, the experiences of life have served to strip women of their rightful place. Instead of joyful, strong, righteous, and valiant women, society has often succeeded in producing anxious, joyless, fearful, pale copies of God's original intention. Yet Jesus promised never to leave us orphans. His Spirit is alive and well, working powerfully against the forces that would destroy his plan for women. Very often women have not been able to say "yes" to God's plan for them because they have been paying too much attention to the voices of the age, believing that these would lead to the Lord's fulfillment.

But God's ways are not ours. His message may not dress itself in the bright and splashy colors displayed by all the new and bold aspects of modern thought; but it more than makes up for them by its richness, its varied hues, its ability to endure, and its power to change us.

We can overcome our feelings of condemnation, anxiety, and bitterness—all the aspects of a miserably poor self-image. The word of God stands firm and unchanging, a beacon over the centuries for those who dare to trust, to believe, to be renewed, and to discover new life.

ONE

Getting Rid of Guilt

Jesus said, "Does anyone ever bring a lamp and put it under a bowl or under the bed? Doesn't he put it on the lampstand? Whatever is hidden away will be brought out into the open, and whatever is covered up will be uncovered" (Mk 4:21-22).

Although placed on the lampstand, our lamps often give little light because for many years they've been covered by layers of cobwebs and dust. One of the most common layers that obscures the light of Christ in our lives is a pervasive sense of guilt.

Have you ever had the experience of walking through your house with your stomach tied in knots, legs of lead, your throat tightly constricted? If you've had these or other symptoms, you may be suffering from "the Big G," or guilt. It may seem to come from nowhere, but when it hits you can feel devastated by it.

Because Jesus came precisely to forgive us and to set us free, our adversary, the devil, works especially hard to make us feel guilty. The good news tells us that we don't have to be weighed down under a mountain of guilt anymore. Knowing this and living in the freedom of it, however, may be two very different things. Let us pray that we may be able to say with Paul: "Let us praise God for his glorious grace, for the free gift he gave us in his dear Son! For by the death of Christ we are set free, that is, our sins are forgiven. How great is the grace of God, which he gave to us in such large measure!" (Eph 1:6-8).

Repent and Be Reconciled

A surprising number of times we may find that we are agonizing in guilt and self-contempt only because it hasn't dawned on us to stop and repent. Sometimes a memory from the distant past may seem more horrible now than before, because the closer we come to the Lord, the darker the evil appears. Our past actions come back to us in greater force when seen in the light of God's goodness. When this happens, we need to turn to the Father quickly to ask his forgiveness. We have God's assurance that he will forgive us if we only turn to him with a repentant heart. God's plan is to set us free, while the enemy's is to force us to become mesmerized by our sinful selves. He wants us to become so tied up in guilt that we forget to lift our heads to the risen Lord to receive the grace he has won for us.

Forgiving Others

In the Gospel of Mark we read, "If you forgive others the wrongs they have done to you, your Father in heaven will also forgive you. But if you do not forgive others, then your Father will not forgive the wrongs you have done" (Mt 6:14-15). These verses point out that we need to forgive others the wrongs they have committed against us. But they also reveal a more subtle truth: if we continue to experience guilt for past sin, it may be that we have not forgiven another who was in some way involved.

Suppose you had a premarital affair and have long since repented, made whatever amends you could, and changed your life. Yet you continue to experience guilt. Have you forgiven the man for his wrongs against you? If not, this could be the cause of your failure to receive the grace of forgiveness in that situation. Once you forgive the man, you will be free to receive forgiveness yourself.

Perhaps your teenager is on drugs or has become pregnant and left home. You have searched your past and repented of any wrongdoing you have committed. Even though you've told yourself that your children have the freedom to choose and the responsibility for the results of their choice, you carry around the "big G" on your chest from the weight of their actions—this apart from the natural pain you would experience as their mother. It may be that your own sense of guilt stems from the fact that you have not forgiven your child. It's impossible to experience the freedom of forgiveness if you are harboring an unforgiving heart. Scripture is clear on this.

If you haven't forgiven someone for their offense, it's important that you go before the Father with a humble and repentant spirit. Consider this: Jesus died for them as well as for you. What does that mean? If you refuse to forgive them, it's as if you refuse to forgive Jesus himself. It's worth remembering in very specific terms the sins that the good God has forgiven you. Suppose, for example, that while you were in the hospital recently, a nurse treated you with great harshness and unkindness. You are still bitter, finding it impossible to forgive her. Consider the times when you have reacted with undo harshness or unkindness to your children or perhaps to your mother or a sister. And God has forgiven you. Can you do less toward another of his children?

Of course, sometimes it is God that we are angry with. If this is the case, we should acknowledge the truth to him and reflect for a time on his great nature—his majesty, might, mercy, and power. We need to remember that he sent his only son out of love for us, knowing that we would ridicule and repudiate him. With this in mind, we can remember who we are in relation to God. We are pretty small potatoes to claim that we deserve better than what God is giving us. We need to repent of a proud heart that insists that our ways are better than God's, our life in need of more comforts than he is providing.

Every time I go before the Lord to receive his forgiveness, I am amazed that he continues to put up with me and to love me. But he does. He is always there, ready to forgive all who ask.

Failure to forgive is not the only reason we may find it difficult to experience forgiveness. Many of us cannot distinguish between real and imagined guilt. Those nauseating, vague feelings of guilt that show up for no apparent reason are distinct from the conviction of the Holy Spirit for a particular action in our lives.

Guilt That Stems from Sin

If we feel guilty because of a particular sin, it's easy to be rid of that guilt. We can repent, ask forgiveness from God and, if possible, of whomever we have injured, do our best to repair any damage we have caused, and resolve to do better by the help of God's grace. If we are truly sorry and have taken these steps to repentance, then we need to stand firm and believe God's word that we are forgiven. If we start to think about what a horrible person we are because of what we have done, we can say, "Well, that's true. But out of his great love, Jesus has borne my sins and taken away my guilt. He has restored me to my place in the Father's house, which he has prepared. He has done this not because I deserve it, but because he is merciful to me, a sinner. I will not deny the power of his death and resurrection by refusing his mercy, but will accept his loving forgiveness into my life."

It's right to experience guilt and the conviction of the Holy Spirit when we have sinned. This kind of guilt is an expression of God's kindness. It motivates us to repent of our wrongdoing and, thus, to be reconciled with him.

Guilt That Stems from Satan and the World

Our experience of guilt often takes the form of condemnation rather than conviction. In this condition, we feel guilty but can determine no apparent cause for the guilt. We may ask the Lord to show us why we feel the way we do, but come up empty. We react by turning our eyes downward and inward. The "Big G" has replaced the cross on our neck chains. We may be so blinded by our own unworthiness that our life with the Lord and with our brothers and sisters suffers greatly.

It's not surprising that this is an area of great difficulty for us. Because Jesus came into the world to set us free, it's to be expected that his enemy and ours—the devil—would do everything possible to make us believe that Jesus' victory was only a sham. The devil cannot change the fact that the victory has been won and that he has been defeated, but as he flees in retreat, he tries to wreak as much havoc as he can. What better way than by trying to convince us that we are beyond the power of the victorious Lord!

Many forces are at work in the world that would try to prevent us from experiencing freedom as sons and daughters of God. This is hardly surprising. Jesus told us that the world that hated him will also hate us. In fact, if the world does not hate us we might be concerned about how well we are living out our Christian commitment. I do not mean that everyone must be against us, but we will be forced to make unpopular decisions and hold unpopular opinions if we believe and act on the word of God. The beliefs of the world are simply incompatible with the truths of the gospel.

At the risk of incurring the world's hatred, I would offer as an example the issue of abortion. I believe that a Christian could not be less than appalled and sickened by the laissez-faire attitude toward abortion that has permeated our society in the last two decades. Though the question of abortion has been surrounded by emotional rhetoric, abortion means killing an innocent life. As Christians we should be outraged, and not afraid of making our opinions known. If we truly believe that we are on God's side in an issue, who are we afraid of? Usually, when we fail to speak up, it's because we fear rejection. If we failed to speak God's word because of fear of rejection, we would incur true guilt that requires repentance. But if we have spoken God's word and, as a result of the world's crazy logic and intimidating rhetoric, are placed in a position where we become the guilty party, then we need to fight off these feelings and stand firm on the word of God. In the case of abortion, scripture is full of references that can sustain us, such as, "You shall not kill" or "Love your neighbor as yourself" (would you have wanted to have been aborted?).

The world puts its own ways and wisdom up against the wisdom, love, and word of God. If we are insecure or unclear on a part of the gospel message and how it should be lived out, then we may feel confused and condemned. We need to study the word of God with the guidance of our church so that we can understand God's mind. We know from Jesus that the world opposed him and will oppose us, too. But when we come up against opposition we often feel guilty for doing what is right! If we recognize that this is happening to us, we ought to talk with a mature Christian about any specific area of confusion, ask the Lord to reveal his mind to us if we are vague about an area, and clear it up in the light of God's word. We should then take a verse from scripture that speaks to the situation and memorize it. When we begin to experience confusion or guilt we can repeat the passage to ourselves as a way of fighting against the pressure to think that any way is better than God's way.

These situations may arise within our own families, sometimes in subtle ways. Husbands may try to make their wives feel guilty; wives may do the same to their husbands; mothers are notorious for doing this to their children; and children are equally adept at attempting this on their mothers.

For example, your five-year-old has taken a magic marker and demonstrated his creativity all over the living-room walls. Your response, appropriately enough, is anger. You give the child a good spanking and have him wash the wall and spend some time in his room. Your child wails and cries out repeatedly, "You don't love me anymore!" As your anger subsides you may begin to have second thoughts about the severity of the punishment. After all, you don't want your child to be warped for life by the experience. So you quiet your thoughts in order to take them to the throne of the Father to whom you must answer for the way you raise your children. You repeat the words he has given you: "Do not let your soul despair for his crying"; or "A good father disciplines the son he loves" (Heb 12:7). Fortified by these words, you can feel confident in your actions, not falling victim to condemnation.

Scapegoating

Another way in which the world pressures us to feel guilty is based on the prevalent practice of scapegoating. People are always pointing their fingers at others, placing blame for every conceivable situation. It's often a mistake to talk in black and white terms about complex situations. Sometimes that is the correct way to approach an issue, but often it isn't. For example, we blame parents for juvenile delinquency, mothers for their son's homosexuality, schools for children's failure to learn, farmers for high food prices, the government for everything from gas prices to unleashed dogs, and the churches for the spiritual state of us all. Of course, each of us affects others by the way we live our lives. And it's often true to say that the fault in one may be largely responsible for the fault in another. If there were not some truth in this we could more easily recognize it as a lie and reject it. Half-truths are harder to catch. They permeate our society.

This half-truth, blame-placing way of speaking pervades our lives and can be very difficult to fight. We might be talking with a fellow passenger on a bus about something as innocuous as the weather. Before we know it, we've fixed the blame for bad weather on big business, for the pollution that is supposedly changing our weather patterns.

The enemy jumps into these situations with both feet, producing two results in us. First, we turn rebellious and resentful of those that we blame and suspicious of everyone else. Second, we begin to feel guilty because if it is true that someone else is responsible for the mess my life is in, then it follows that I must be responsible for the mess someone else's life is in.

We can do a few things to correct this situation. We can control our speech to make sure that we aren't contributing to the problem of indiscriminately placing blame on others. We can ask God to show us when we are accepting blame that doesn't belong to us. And we can *sort things out*.

Sorting through Our Guilt

By sorting things out I mean that we should look at all the facets of the situation in the light of God's love, admit to any wrongdoing on our part, repent, and forgive anyone else for their wrongdoing. *Sorting things out* is such a worthwhile tool that I would like to share several examples in some detail to demonstrate how this can work in our lives to set us free.

Because women have responsibility for the home environment, we are particularly vulnerable in this area, and often assume that we are guilty for another's actions. While our children are small they depend on us completely, and even as they grow more independent physically, their need for our nurture is probably even stronger in certain ways. With so much depending on us, it's easy to become a convenient receptacle for everyone's guilt. More often than not we accept the blame without question.

Case 1: I have a friend whose son was just a toddler when he stumbled and fell while walking in the house. He cried so much that she picked him up to comfort him, but he only cried louder, even after she had rocked him and prayed with him. Because he continued to be distressed, she brought him to the doctor and discovered that he had broken his leg. Of course the mother felt horrible. And she had to fight off guilt by sorting things out with the truth: "My house is not set up like an obstacle course. All toddlers stumble as they learn to walk. I could not have prevented it. If I missed praying for the children's protection for a day or two, I know that God loves them even more than I do and is merciful. He is even now protecting them from some greater harm."

In this situation, no one was at fault, and the mother had to fight off guilt with the truth.

Case 2: Suppose your son complains that you are starving him and forcing him to use money from his paper route to buy food because your meals are so bad. Food can be one of the most difficult issues in a home, but we can still use the technique of sorting things out to help clear up this type of situation. You may become angry if your son speaks to you in this way, but a little bit of guilt begins to creep into your spirit as well. To sort it out, consider these things.

Are you preparing nutritious meals? If not, you should repent and begin to do so. Probably you are, however, but unless you are serving a hamburger and fries or a pizza, it is not a meal to your son. Are you making an effort to provide meals that your husband and others in the family like? If so, don't accept the guilt that your son's accusations causes. Instead, correct him for being disrespectful, point out the truth to him, and forgive him thereby keeping the root of bitterness from growing within you. Take the "G" off your chest and throw it away, realizing that if your son spends his hard-earned money on other food, that is *his* choice, not yours.

Case 3: Suppose your six-month-old baby has a bad case of diaper rash. You've taken her to the doctor, who has prescribed medication and changed her diet in an attempt to check for food allergies. You are already feeling bad enough when a friend tells you the baby's rash resulted from your decision not to nurse the baby, but to bottle-feed her instead. You may feel resentful and angry upon hearing these words, but you will probably feel guilty as well. How do you get rid of the guilt? Look at the facts.

Quality of care is not based on breast- or bottle-feeding. You have cared for your child in a very good way by seeking medical help when lotions alone did not cure the rash. Your friend is not qualified to make a medical judgment and has offered an opinion for which no confirmation is at hand. You might mention your distress to your friend to help her see the pain it caused, depending upon your relationship with her. You need, at least, to forgive her for accusing you, in essence, of being a bad mother. And you need to ask God for the grace to believe that love really does cover a multitude of sins. If you have any nagging guilt left about your decision to nurture your child in a particular way, it has been more than covered over by love.

Case 4: Your husband comes downstairs in the morning barefoot and holding his shoes. He is angry because he cannot find any socks, and accuses you of putting so many other priorities ahead of him that he cannot even leave the house with clean socks. You feel angry and guilty. Let's sort it out.

Your husband should be able to have clean socks in his drawer in the morning. If your week has been such a nightmare that you absolutely could not get to the wash (perhaps you have spent most of your days and nights in the hospital staying with a sick child), then you might have an excuse. If not, your anger or defensiveness to your husband's reaction is probably unjustified, and you need to repent, ask forgiveness, and change your priorities. Then you will be free from guilt.

Case 5: Your husband needs to leave the house by 6:45 to be at work on time. He has asked that you never shut off the alarm for him, so that he will be sure to get up. He turns off the alarm and goes back to sleep on this particular day while you are downstairs fixing breakfast. Realizing that it's getting late, you go up to check and find him still asleep. He dresses hurriedly, has no time for breakfast, and angrily accuses you of not getting him up on time. You react with guilt, confusion, and some anger. Sorting it out, you realize that you didn't turn off the alarm; you had done as he asked. Although you did all that was required, perhaps you might have listened more closely for his footsteps upstairs to ascertain if he was indeed up. You might resolve to be a little more attentive in the future. But, ultimately, your husband is responsible for getting himself out of bed, and you should not accept the blame. You should go before the Lord, forgive your husband for trying to blame you, and ask him to prevent you from carrying that guilt around all day.

The Holy Spirit is our great friend and comforter, who brings us wisdom for these and many other circumstances. He acts within us to make us more righteous, to teach us to follow Jesus to the glory of God the Father. God did not leave us orphans and is concerned to give us everything that is for our greater good. Certainly our freedom to live as sons and daughters of God is both for our good and for the honor and glory of God.

The Problem of Pride

Besides the fact that our families depend on us in such a way that we can become receptacles for their guilt, there are two other reasons why we accept guilt so easily: a poor self-image and pride. I'll have more to say about self-image later. Pride is a persistent problem for us. If we stop and consider, we'll be amazed to realize that it's our ego that motivates us to think that everything is our fault. We can get carried away, believing that we are responsible for everything from the dog's bad breath to the breakdown of the washing machine, from the rain that spoiled the picnic (didn't pray hard enough) to our daughter's abortion. We need to repent of that kind of pride. We ought to be quick to repent, quick to forgive, and quick to accept forgiveness.

If some things I have said so far have made you feel crummy about yourself, guilty of being prideful, just stop a minute and ask the Lord to help you sort out this area of your life. Remember, if you are guilty of wrongdoing, it can be righted. Just repent and make it right. Then accept Jesus' forgiveness, making sure you have also forgiven others the wrongs they have done. Remember that God himself has died for you and loved you while you were still in your sins. You cannot hide your sinfulness from him or pretend that it doesn't exist. He loves you anyway. That's why he gave his life for you—to free you from such bondage. If you feel guilty because the enemy is telling you that you are a terrible person, resist him. You may be a sinner, but Jesus loves you even now. He comes not with condemnation, but with mercy. You are no more in need of a savior than anyone else, for we are all weak and sinful before God's glory. Let us rely, therefore, not on our own strength, which in most cases is weakness, but on the strength of the risen Savior that in every case is victorious.

Our Righteousness Comes from God

Another reason for the condemnation we experience stems from the fact that we try so hard to do what is right and fail. St. Paul spoke about this conflict in Romans. "We know that the Law is spiritual; but I am a mortal man, sold as a slave to sin. I do not understand what I do; for I don't do what I would like to do, but instead I do what I hate" (7:14-15).

We also read that we should obey the law and, elsewhere, that we are set free from it. This can cause confusion and guilt for us, which is clearly not God's plan for our lives. Of course, it is good and useful for us to know our unworthiness before

God. But this does not mean that we should be tied up in knots of confusion regarding these matters.

Let us briefly consider a few of the many passages of scripture that speak of the law. In Matthew, Jesus says that he has not come to do away with the law "but to make theirthe law and the prophetsteachings come true" (5:17). He continues, "So then, whoever disobeys even the least important of the commandments and teaches others to do the same, will be least in the Kingdom of heaven. On the other hand, whoever obeys the Law and teaches others to do the same, will be great in the Kingdom of heaven. I tell you, then, that you will be able to enter the Kingdom of heaven only if you are more faithful than the teachers of the Law and the Pharisees in doing what God requires" (Mt 5:19-20).

That's an astonishing statement. The Pharisees were more scrupulous in their observance of the law than the average person could ever hope to be. How could we be more faithful?

The answer to this question can be found by posing another: What does God require? According to scripture, the two most important commandments are to 'Love the Lord your God with all your heart, with all your soul, and with all your mind' and to 'Love your neighbor as you love yourself.' The whole Law of Moses and the teachings of the prophets depend on these two commandments" (Mt 22:37-40).

Obviously, the Pharisees' attention to detail, their attempt to master each intricacy of the law did not necessarily help them to love God and their neighbor more, which was the very core of the law. What went wrong, and what hope is there for us? The answer can be seen quite dramatically in Paul's letter to the Philippians. Paul enumerates the many ways he was zealous in doing what the law required but goes on to say that he counts all that as refuse so that he may "gain Christ and be completely united with him." He has the "righteousness that is *given* through faith in Christ, the righteousness that *comes from God* and is based on faith" (Phil 3:8-9). According to Paul he has been made righteous by God; his righteousness does not stem from himself. Knowing this, we might expect that Paul would sit back complacently, waiting for the Lord to come. Yet two verses later comes the famous passage about "striving to win the prize" (Phil 3:12).

Paul works even harder than when he tried to be perfect in obeying the law. How is this possible? He gives us the answer when he says, "So I run straight toward the *goal* in order to win the *prize,* which is God's call through Christ Jesus to the life above" (Phil 13:14).

Do you see it yet? We are all runners, like Paul. When we become bound up with confusion and guilt, it is often because we are trying to do what is right on our own strength. The more we try to do the right thing, scrutinizing our every move, the more defeated we seem to become. Paul admitted that his own righteousness was non-existent. He was a sinner at God's mercy, who counted on God's righteousness. Second, he kept his eyes off of his feet and placed them on his goal—on unity with Jesus forever—the greatest prize of all.

An attitude like Paul's takes the pressure off us. It's true that we must strive with all our strength, but we do it with our heads up, intent on the goal. Any jogger knows that you cannot run very well by looking at your feet. You would be running into things constantly. By looking ahead to your goal, which gets closer and closer, you are spurred to greater effort.

We can deal with this kind of guilt and confusion by repenting of the pride which tries to win salvation by our own efforts and our own righteousness in "following the law." We must ask for the grace to accept the Spirit of God and his righteousness, that our strivings may always be toward Jesus and in Jesus.

By this, I don't mean to imply that we are exempt from the law. It is just that our goal is no longer "obedience," though we need to obey—or "wisdom," though we need to be wise, or "righteousness," though we ought to be righteous. Nor should our goal be to acquire purity, peace, patience, fortitude, endurance, and fear of the Lord, though these qualities should characterize our lives as Christians. Our goal is Jesus; our way is Jesus; our truth is Jesus. Life itself is Jesus. It is futile to try to reach the Father by our own efforts, according to our plan, our timetable, and our power. If that were possible, we would not need a savior. But Jesus did come to take us home to his Father. That knowledge can bring us the confidence and freedom to strive for greater and greater love—that our lives may be filled with the desire to do only the will of God.

If you are experiencing the conviction of the Holy Spirit regarding these things, please do not feel crushed by guilt. Rather, rejoice that you can repent and ask God to do the rest. His mercy is limitless, his forgiveness boundless, and his love beyond anything we can imagine. Remember always, he came to set us free, that we may have life itself and have it abundantly. He is life. Let us do away with condemnation and guilt. With a humble and contrite spirit let us say yes to the work of Jesus, who sets us free.

If we can begin to let Jesus do this work in our lives, we may begin to notice a glow that comes from deep within our prisms. We will begin to reflect the freedom of the risen Savior himself.

TWO

Letting Our Self-Image Be Polished

One of the hardest prisms to restore is the one called "self-image." For every one of us, life holds its share of difficulties. In the midst of our hurt, we have chosen different weapons and defenses to help us survive. Once we discover that God himself will protect us, we may be relieved, but still puzzled. Do we dare entrust ourselves to another? Where do we begin to trust the Father's love? What elements of our personalities and reactions reflect God's plan for our lives, and what elements require healing and growth? How do we begin to give ourselves to God?

Some of us respond to hurt by standing our ground and constructing a strong defensive wall around ourselves. Others of us accept abuse as though it's a true measure of our self-worth. We've concluded that we're pretty worthless individuals. Some of us may think that we can handle anything, and others feel that one more hurt will do us in.

No one answer to all these questions will suffice. Everyone's life is unique. Even so, I've struggled with these difficulties in my own life, and know that God can lead us from confusion and doubt to a place of real peace. The Lord is gracious, and we can count on his steadfast love. He wants to bring only good into our lives and out of our lives. He has a plan for us in hard times as well as good times. But before we can believe that this is true, God will have to work a series of quiet miracles in our inmost being, with our cooperation.

Scripture and the kindness of our brothers and sisters make the truth of God's love for us a reality in our lives. As I share ways the Lord has worked in my life and in the lives of others, I hope you will be encouraged to open your own life to the healing touch of the risen Savior. Our Father wants us to view ourselves as his daughters, living in the courts of the great King. As his daughters we are confident that his love can overpower our self-concern, leaving us free to love others in return. God plans to accomplish this work in each one of us.

Our Cross: Made with Us in Mind

Like many people, I grew up without a strong self-image, though there were no major traumas in my life to produce this result. Because of this I've learned not to judge my cross in relation to others. All of our crosses are made with us in mind. One person's cross could be another's joy. For instance, some people may find it difficult to live in a large city, while others love the excitement and variety provided by big city life.

Sometimes our joy can also be our cross. Five children may be a great blessing, but when the oldest is only seven, their mother will have little time to reflect on that. The demands made upon her at this time will be a cross for her.

So don't feel guilty if you've had a hard time of it even though your cross doesn't look very big. Each cross is made to suit the person. It's essential to learn to carry the cross in the right way—to accept the lot that God has given you, to learn to rejoice in the situation, and to overcome the hurts with the help of Jesus.

"Rejoice always,"—scripture makes us confident that it is possible to be at peace and full of the Lord's joy in the midst of trials. Of course it would be foolish to expect that rejoicing will be our natural response to difficulty. Without Jesus, it doesn't make sense to rejoice. We've had to expend a lot of time and energy just learning how to survive. Rejoicing in the midst of trial comes only by God's grace. Our joy isn't based on the actual difficulty, but on God: "Let your *hope* keep you joyful, be patient in your troubles, and pray at all times" (Rom 12:12). If you want to learn to be a happy, joyful person while carrying your cross, this is the key.

Helping Each Other through the Hard Times

St. Paul tells us to "Be happy with those who are happy, weep with those who weep" (Rom 12:15). While our hope should keep us from despair, it is also true that everyone experiences seasons of sorrow, hurt, and disappointment. We need to help one another through these. This kind of approach can free women struggling with a poor self-image. Let me explain.

Many women tend to feel isolated while in a crowd. They feel as though they've behaved or talked like a boor while attending a social gathering. If they are really anxious about it, they may even feel like crawling in a hole or leaving town rather than facing people. Even though many women, and probably a lot of men, experience this type of anxiety, almost everyone thinks that their problem is unique. As they observe the behavior of others, they conclude that it is superior to their own in most cases. Yet, when two friends begin to share their difficulty, they will be amazed that they both struggle with this area. They see that their anxiety is not unique; in fact it is shared by someone who seems very much at ease in a social gathering. If that's so, then there's hope that their conduct, too, has been appropriate to the situation. When Christian women share in this way, they can pray for and encourage one another.

Whenever I experienced this type of anxiety in a social setting, I would tell my husband about my frustrations when I got home. He would ask me specific questions about what I actually said or did that I considered wrong or stupid. As I responded, he would say, "No, that was fine," or, "You should have been more considerate," or "Maybe next time you could do this instead of that, but forget it for now." This made the evening much easier to deal with. Instead of letting vague, nauseous feelings about what a lousy person I was take over, I could do something concrete. It wasn't easy being truthful with myself or my husband, but I soon learned to look at my behavior more objectively, without always having his help.

Some of us may not be able to share like this with our husbands. Or we may be single and suffer from the same anxieties. But we can at least talk things over with Jesus. When we pray, we can ask the Father for his wisdom. We can claim his love. We should be quick to repent, to ask and receive forgiveness. If we have been offended, we must be quick to forgive others, and quick to ask the Lord to love us in the midst of our hurt.

Don't become discouraged if you don't experience God's love and peace immediately. It can take time and effort, especially in cases where the distress goes deep. It's taken years to become the person you are today, and it will take a while to become the new creation that God is bringing into being. Knowing that God loves you, that you're a daughter of the King, will enable you to think of others' needs in any kind of social setting. As you forget about yourself, you will become less self-conscious and more conscious of God and others.

When you're tempted to become discouraged at how long it's taking for the "new woman" to emerge, think about Lazarus. When Jesus called Lazarus from the tomb, he received new life and was transformed into a new creation in a very real sense. But he must have looked awful in his burial wrappings. Even his face must have been covered. Jesus told those around him: "Untie him and let him go." We, too, have been set free and have become new creations by the power of the risen Lord. But, like Lazarus, we come stumbling out into the light and need help to get the wrappings off.

To Be a Woman

Why do many women perceive themselves so negatively? The answer is tied in part with how we first began to view womanhood, and how we first experienced ourselves changing from a girl to a woman. Puberty can be a very confusing and bewildering time. Acutely conscious of their changing bodies, young girls are apt to compare themselves with others, even those who may be many years older. At this age, children can be extremely thoughtless and cruel in their remarks to and about others. Young girls find that their emotions are hard to deal with, their friendships seem tenuous, and their relationships with their parents suffer as they struggle between remaining a child one minute and entering the adult world the next. This happens just when they need their parents most, especially their mothers. We need to double our prayers for our daughters during this difficult time and to work especially hard at keeping the lines of communication open.

Although I had many positive expectations about womanhood, I remember a couple of crude comments another girl made to me about my figure. Too hurt to tell my mother about this episode, I responded by becoming stoop-shouldered, thinking that if I could hide my developing figure I would appear to be a more humble person. This incident made me suspect that it was not all that desirable to become a woman. However, since most of my experiences were positive, I moved into adulthood without much trouble. Even so, this incident came to mind frequently after I began to experience a closer relationship with the Lord. Finally it dawned on me that I needed to forgive the girl who had said those things. Only then could I expect healing for that area of my life.

I did this, recalling a few other incidents where I needed to forgive others and to repent myself. It seemed as though the Father had just been waiting for this to happen. Not long afterwards, I began to experience healing in this area of my life. Gradually I became more comfortable with my body and my womanhood. I knew also that God had made both men and women and that women were a beautiful part of his plan for creation. I began to see how the Bible honored outstanding women. Mary had been granted the greatest privilege ever given—to become the mother of God. And Mary Magdalene was the first to see Jesus risen. There was dignity in being a woman.

Women: Strengths for God's Kingdom

It has become increasingly fashionable to assert that the only differences that exist between men and women are biological ones. This trend runs counter to the practices and beliefs of Christians throughout the centuries. Scripture indicates clearly that role distinctions between men and women are important, though there is no distinction between them in terms of their worth in God's sight and their access to salvation.

One could say that biological differences express the way our role as women differs from that of men. Even as we nurture life within the womb, making a home for a baby for nine months of intense growth, so our function in the home environment is to nurture life and promote growth. The same can be said even of women who are single, who may not have responsibility for the overall care of a home. Most single women, whatever their home environment, take time to beautify it, to create a place where life can be lived more fully. In work environments, too, women try to do what they can to make a place more livable, whether it means adding plants, pictures, or nicknacks or whether it means expending more effort towards strengthening relationships.

All these things are a sign of our womanhood. They add to our dignity as women of God. We aren't perfect, and we don't share the same personalities and approaches to problems. But we are all concerned with the quality of life and are apt to invest our energies to maintain and improve that quality. That doesn't mean that men are never concerned about these things, but that women tend to possess these concerns to a high degree. Those of us with husbands and homes can view our role as helpmate with great pride and gratitude. It's not a role that degrades us, but one that can be a tool for developing great strength as well as a kind and firm spirit within us. To be a good and true helpmate, a woman cannot afford to remain weak. For a building to stand, it must rest on strong supports. The same is true for our role as a support to our husbands and families. God builds on our strengths, not our weaknesses.

But what if you've got to be both a mother and father in the home? Remember that God offers great mercy; he will supply what you lack. Anyone would be inadequate in this situation. Don't grow discouraged and lose your confidence in what God has been doing in you. Do the best you can, knowing that you are not made to be both a man and a woman, but that God will provide for your children in ways you cannot.

Self-Respect Comes from God

Our self-image must be based on the truth, and Jesus Christ is the truth. Therefore, it's important to view yourself as Jesus sees you. A friend of mine reminded me once that Jesus sees us as we will be in glory. He is not bound by time as we are. Christ is not deluded about our present, imperfect state. This is clear from the gospel account. He died for us while we were still sinners, and his love doesn't depend on our righteousness or lovableness. If it did, none of us could hope to be loved by him. "A person can never redeem himself; he cannot pay God the price for his life, because the payment for a human life is too great. What he could pay would never be enough to keep him from the grave, to let him live forever" (Ps 49:7-9).

On our own we are helpless. We can do nothing. But from his boundless mercy and love, Jesus has won for us a place in the Father's house.

Intellectually you may be convinced that this is true, but how can this knowledge make a difference in your life? Consider this. Suppose that all morning you have been especially aware of God's love for you. At noon, a friend drops by and tells you that a thoughtless remark that you made to her the previous day hurt her badly. Feeling ashamed, you ask your friend's forgiveness. When she leaves, you begin to feel yourself the worst of sinners, unworthy to go before the Father to ask his forgiveness. All morning you had been experiencing God's love even though he knew that you had wronged your friend the day before. Nothing has changed except that now you know your sin also. God's love toward you hasn't diminished. Only your perception of yourself has changed. God's love is constant. His love is the same yesterday, today, and tomorrow.

You can rely on that truth when you ask God's forgiveness, repenting of the wrong you have done.

Act Like You're Loved

Sometimes our feelings assure us that God loves us. But regardless of how we feel, we ought to *act* as if his love and mercy are constant because scripture says that they are. As we begin to act on this truth, the Spirit will begin to work the reality into our hearts. Let me give you an example. Suppose I'm caring for my children in the right way but *feel* like the world's most inadequate mother. I need to remember the truth. God has given me these children, and he will not test me beyond my strength. Even if I can't care for them on my own strength, I can do all things in him. In my weakness God's glory will be manifest. With this in mind, I can proceed with the cares of the day with the confidence of a daughter of the King. I can put aside my own view of my life to take on God's view and to rely on his strength. I needn't wait until all the children are either gone or napping before asking the Lord for his truth and his help. I can do this while washing my face, brushing my teeth, dressing, or preparing breakfast. I have been known on occasion to stay in bed another minute or two in order to pray in this way, if I have awakened discouraged. It helps at a time like this to thank God for the life he has chosen for us, the children he has given us, and most especially for himself.

It can sometimes help to read scripture as if you were the one spoken to or the one healed. If you read a story about healing, make an act of faith: "Jesus wants to heal me in the same way." You can read about Jesus' compassion for the crowds and say, "I'm in the crowd, too. Jesus has the same compassion on me." You can read Jesus' prayer to the Father at the Last Supper and say, "Jesus was praying for me, too." That's the truth. You may think that Jesus died for everybody but you; you are much too horrible a person to be worthy of salvation. But who among us is worthy? St. Paul assures us that none of us are. That's the whole point. That's why we can hope for salvation—not because we are worthy, but because Christ is.

Fortunately Jesus did not stop at dying for us. He sent his Spirit to set about the business of restoring all our parts to working order. I like to view myself as that prism lamp that shines brightly from within because of the salvation that Jesus has won for me. The Spirit's role is to polish, clean, and occasionally repair the lamp. We ought to help one another with the polishing and cleaning. But it takes God's Spirit to restore a prism so that no crack can be detected by even the strongest light.

While we must acknowledge our unworthiness and our complete dependence upon God for our salvation and our righteousness, at the same time we are called to see ourselves as he sees us in glory. Sometimes we may fear becoming prideful. But our understanding of God's greatness and our weakness in relation to him will surely keep us humble. We can ask the Father to help us shed our defenses in order to depend on him for everything. For that is the great contradiction of our faith: in order to have life, we must die. In order to be truly strong we must be completely dependent upon God. Our joy comes from knowing that Jesus has gone before us and has already won the victory. As we empty ourselves of everything that is not of him, we can be filled with his Spirit.

It isn't our goodness or righteousness that people respond to; it's God living in us, attracting others to himself. As this truth gets worked into our hearts, we won't fear becoming prideful. We will be glad to see our will decrease to be replaced by God's will. We dare to consider ourselves worthy, not because of who we are but because of who God is. Once we know this, we'll grow in respect for all of God's children.

Most of us have had the experience of meeting someone in whose presence we experience the very real presence of God. It usually leads us closer to the Father. We may want to get to know that person better so that we can learn how to empty ourselves of that which is not God in order to make room for him. So let us not be afraid to become a person like that, to let the light of God shine through us. If it is God's light and God's love that we are reflecting, it can only bring good.

Negative Speech

Christian women can make the mistake of confusing humiliation with humility. In an effort to practice humility, they may have gotten in the habit of making negative comments about themselves in front of others. But this is really false humility. They may have learned not to gossip and may endeavor to speak well of others and to encourage them. But when the conversation turns to them, they criticize or make fun of themselves, sometimes even stretching the truth in order to avoid seeming proud. This kind of behavior actually focuses more attention on themselves since others will attempt to assure them that they are better than they claim. This can result in awkward and strained relationships.

But the problem can go even deeper. We have no more right to badmouth ourselves than to badmouth anyone else in the body of Christ. God does not want to hear any of his daughters slandered. We should strive to show ourselves the courtesy of proper speech. Of course, we needn't go out of our way to brag about our accomplishments or to demand honor for our achievements. But neither should we deny or be ashamed to admit that God is changing and forming us into a new creation.

If someone compliments us, we should simply say "Thank you" instead of "Oh, I'm sure someone else could have done a better job." If another woman was complimented in our presence for the same thing, we would certainly not make such a negative remark about her performance!

A while ago, God showed me something else about showing proper respect toward myself. One of my ideals has been to leave a place in which I've worked in better condition than when I entered it, out of love for those who would go there after me. But since most of my work is done in my home, I felt that I could not apply that principle very often.

One night I was rushing to clean up the kitchen after dinner. It was quite late, and I was not in the mood to do a great job.

"What does it matter, anyway," I thought. "I'm the one who will have to face this and clean up in the morning." Then I remembered my ideal about cleaning up for the next person out of love. I also recalled that I was supposed to act respectfully toward myself. I realized that God was asking me to love myself enough to clean up the kitchen well so that I could face my morning with a lighter heart. If someone else was going to prepare breakfast the following morning I wouldn't have left a messy kitchen but would have gone out of my way to set out cereal bowls, plates, silverware—whatever would ease the task. I began to do this for myself, even though I did not *feel* like I was worth it. Yet, as I strove to apply this principle over the next few months, it helped me to think better of myself. Because I was conscious of respecting myself as one of God's daughters, I was better able to show honor and respect toward others. Instead of dwelling on what a crummy person I was, I was able to concern myself with acting on God's word and doing his will.

Building on Strength

If we speak negatively about ourselves or fail to show ourselves respect, we are really concentrating on our weakness rather than God's strength. As a result we'll be much more susceptible to lies from the enemy about ourselves, and thus more likely to sin. As we begin to speak and act with more respect toward ourselves, we will begin to view ourselves from a position of strength. We will be able to ask for God's mercy and help, confident that he will give it. Our plan should be to put on the whole armor of God, not only for defense, but as the best offense for the sake of God's glory. Introspection makes us rely on others to hold the armor in front of us. Of course it's important to rely on other Christians for strength and protection. But God wants us to firmly grasp the strength he has won for us. Jesus wants us to be able to accept our weaknesses and strengths, to offer our whole self to him to be changed into the women he wants us to be. He wants us to think of doing his will alone, instead of filling our thoughts with self-condemnation. God wants us whole.

I would like to say a word about anger here. Sometimes it is assumed that angry people are strong people. After all, they aren't afraid to express themselves, even if it means hurting another. Actually, many people who have a poor self-image also have a problem with anger. If we think there's any truth in some negative comment, joke, or correction, our reaction will often be one of anger. If we have a poor self-image, we will be getting angry a great deal. Of course our anger may be a symptom of pride. However, such situations can make us angry because we fear that others will know how horrible we really are if we allow ourselves to admit a fault. We strive to convince people that we are right because we have a deep fear of being wrong. This kind of behavior prevents us from repenting and receiving forgiveness—the only means for restoring our self-image. We should pray for the humility to admit when we are wrong and to be grateful for correction as an opportunity to learn. It's OK not to be perfect as long as we do not intend to remain in our sin.

Rooted in God's Image

Our self-image should be based on God's view of us rather than on our view or that of others. In fact, a better name for our self-image would be God's image. Let me explain. Suppose you enjoy being around people. It makes you feel happy and loved. You're always the last to leave a party. But when you think about it, you realize that the love and admiration others have for you lulls you into thinking well of yourself. You are loathe to leave the party and face your own poor self-image. You may have been able to fool those at the party, you reason, but you cannot face yourself with the ugly truth of who you really are. You may even feel that if these same friendly people ever discovered the real you, they would never want to see you again.

The astounding truth is that Jesus does know the real us. In fact, he knows us better than we know ourselves. As Paul says, "What I know now is only partial; then it will be complete—as complete as God's knowledge of me" (1 Cor 13:12). And yet God loves us. Viewing ourselves in God's image means that we will accept the fact that we are lovable. If we deny this, we deny God and his plan for us. We are lovable because God loved us first.

Knowing this and living it can be two different things. We need to act with the certainty that we are loved even when we do not particularly feel that way. It's important to act in this way when surrounded by people who love us, but it's even more important when surrounded by people who do not seem to love us. Our confidence must be in God, not in the circumstances. If we lack this confidence and fail to remember that we are God's daughters, we will be caught in the snare of temptations that the enemy sets for us. If, however, we act from a position of strength, as someone loved, then we are free to forget about ourselves and our need for honor or affection. We become free to love and honor others, demonstrating our love and affection for them. When love, affection, and honor come our way, we will be able to accept them, secure in the knowledge that it is God's work that others are responding to.

It is so refreshing to give up the pride that thinks only of self. We can begin to ask others about their interests without putting ours first. We can look for ways to compliment others rather than worrying about how we look or how we will be received. We accept others because we will not be so worried about being accepted. We can in all things seek first to please and serve God instead of ourselves. We can be kind to others for their sake and the sake of the Lord

It Takes Time

This takes a lot of effort on our part, probably over a period of years. Let us not grow discouraged, falling into negative thinking about ourselves. Instead, let us turn our discouragement into rejoicing. When we get to the end of our strength we can rejoice, because now we will be relying entirely on God's strength. When we get to the end of our ability to love we can rejoice, because now we can love with God's own love, which is so much greater than our own. When we get to the end of our patience, we can rejoice that now we can grow in using the Lord's patience. In fact why wait? Why not start depending on God in all things now? If we fail, we can be quick to repent and quick to receive forgiveness. Jesus is faithful, even when we are not. He knows it will take us time to grow.

But what if we still are discontented about facets of our personality? This discontent often stems from two sources: failing to accept our lot and comparing ourselves with others. These two sources of discontent are closely related. When we don't like our lives, someone else's will always look better to us. But envy and discontent can be terribly destructive to ourselves and to the body of Christ. Whenever we begin to think along those lines, we should stop and repent quickly. Then we should give thanks to the living God for his love and mercy and for the lot he has given to us.

Paul tells us in 1 Corinthians that we are all a body in Christ, and that if we were all an eye, we would not be a body. An eye without the rest of the body cannot see. A body without feet cannot walk. A body without hands cannot accomplish much. A body without a heart, quietly pumping away, would lie lifeless. Whatever part of the body we are, seen or unseen, we are there for the sake of the others, through our head, Jesus Christ. Let us not strive to be something different than what God is calling us to be. Let us be the best we can wherever we are, strong enough to move on when the Lord calls. Let us do all this in the knowledge that we are loved and are lovable, so that God's light may glow in us, reflecting his glory and drawing others to himself.

THREE

A Grateful Heart Drives Out Bitterness

A friend of mine told me recently about an experience she had when she was a fairly new Christian. The first joy and closeness to the Lord that she had experienced seemed to have vanished mysteriously. God seemed very far away, and she longed to have him near again. She remembers standing at the foot of her bed one night and crying out in her pain, "Oh, God! Where have you gone?"

As she stood there, she began to picture a heavy cable attached to her and leading upward toward heaven. But as she gazed upward she noticed that something like a garbage can cover hung halfway between, much as a metal disc on a ship's ropes that is designed to keep animals off the vessel. As she was wondering about the reason for the cover she had a sense that the Lord was saying, "This is your resentment and bitterness. It stands between us. You cannot get past it to come closer to me; and my love cannot get past it to come closer to you, for you have placed it there between us."

My friend's grace-filled response was to repent. "Nothing is worth so high a price," she told me years later, "especially something so ugly as resentment." Over the years, when tempted to hold onto bitterness, she would remember this incident. Realizing that resentment created obstructions in her relationship with God, she would choose life and unity with the Father instead.

My friend's experience points out graphically the destructiveness of bitterness. It will undermine the very foundation of our life with God. It will also do the same with other relationships. Scripture says, "Guard against turning back from the grace of God. Let no one become like a bitter plant that grows up and causes many troubles with its poison" (Heb 12:15). Another translation says, "See to it . . . that no 'root of bitterness' spring up and cause trouble" (12:15).

The Difference between Anger and Bitterness

It helps to distinguish between anger and bitterness. Anger can sometimes be the right response to a situation. When faced with injustice and wrongdoing we ought to be angry and respond appropriately to the situation. Bitterness involves bearing grudges against others. Perhaps it began with justified anger that later got out of control or that did not admit of forgiveness. Or it may have stemmed from situations in which our feelings have been hurt or some imagined slight has been given. We continue to dwell on the offense and build upon it. Let me offer an example to clarify this.

A friend of mine with two children, aged nine and seven, discovered that she was pregnant again. She and her husband were delighted at the prospect of another child and shared the good news with their children. The nine-year-old was especially excited about the pregnancy. Because her own body was preparing for the changes that would be bringing her along the path to womanhood, she was particularly sensitive to all the changes in her mother's body. When her mother was four months pregnant, the daughter shared the news with a neighbor girl and her mother. The other child's mother launched into a tirade about the inadvisability of a pregnancy at her mother's age (thirty-one!). She talked about the high rate of deformity among infants born to older women, the problem with overpopulation, and so on. Of course the child was terribly upset by this. Despite her mother's attempts to calm her fears, she became very anxious about her mother and the baby's health throughout the remainder of the pregnancy.

My friend's response was to become righteously angry with

her neighbor. She had wittingly or unwittingly placed a terribly heavy burden on the back of a nine-year-old. After all, her neighbor had no business interfering in this way. So she told her neighbor of the trauma she had caused and asked her to try to repair the damage that she had done.

The neighbor didn't ask for forgiveness, nor was she very cooperative about helping to repair the damage. My friend was then faced with two choices. She could hold on to her anger, allowing it to fester within her and perhaps to color other areas of her life; or she could ask the Lord for the grace to forgive the woman, giving up what she felt was justified anger.

The anger had been righteous, and my friend's response was correct. But to hold on to her anger until it destroyed her would have been wrong. She needed to let go of it. By God's grace she was able to. Even so, every time her daughter expressed her fears, she found that she had to ask the Lord again for the grace to be able to forgive. Since the neighbor made no attempt at reparation, my friend took care to see that her daughter didn't spend much time at the neighbor's house and that she didn't discuss her mother's pregnancy with her.

In my experience bitterness is a terribly easy temptation to give in to, one whose effects are hard to undo. It is one of the most destructive weapons in the devil's arsenal. We may see the danger but still feel helpless in the face of resentment. We want our lamps to burn brightly and know that resentment acts like a dark cloak of dirt covering the light. But how do we get rid of it? How do we begin to even want to forgive someone for wounds that still fester? How do we deal with that vast reservoir of hurts? How do we keep hurts and bitterness from destroying our new life with Jesus and with our friends and families? How do we face the fact that sometimes we resent God himself? If we find it difficult to overcome resentment against God, who is perfect, how can we hope to stop feeling resentful towards the ungodly?

As always, God is our hope. He wouldn't command us to "forgive others as I have forgiven you" without giving us the power to accomplish the impossible. For it is impossible to forgive as the Lord forgives without the spirit of God, who enables us to do all things in Christ, who has gone before us. God knows that our failure to forgive will bring about our death. Bitterness has no part in God's life and should have no part in ours. We can be assured that God will supply every grace that we need to overcome bitterness.

Resentment against God

Let us consider first whether we hold any resentment against God. At different times in our lives, we may find that we are holding many things against him: that a loved one has died, that someone is sick or suffering, that we have to work in the home and cannot get out very often, that we have to work outside the home, that our unmarried daughter has become pregnant, that our son is in trouble with the law, that our husband objects to our conversion to Christ, that we do not yet have a husband. These situations and more can cause real anguish in our lives. And it can be a comfort for the Christian to know that there will be a better life to come. But even in this life, we can make unscriptural responses to difficulties, which make life more painful. What do I mean by this? Let me give you an example.

Suppose your teenage daughter starts to feel ill and misses a few days of school. You both know how hard it will be to make up the time missed, and you begin to feel tense about it. In the next few weeks she misses even more time and becomes very depressed, thinking that she may be in danger of failing the semester. The doctor can find no immediate solution to her medical difficulties. Now you're losing money as well as time. You begin to suspect that your daughter's illness may be emotional rather than physical. Though you try to encourage her, her condition remains the same, and you grow weary and discouraged. Your frustration wells up until it turns into anger. Your daughter feels bad enough as it is, so you don't want to direct your anger against her. The doctor can't really be blamed for not knowing the cause of your daughter's sickness. You are tempted to be angry with yourself for not doing more for your daughter. After all, you are her mother and have grown used to wearing the big "G." In the midst of this struggle you have the nagging feeling that it's all somehow unfair. It's unfair to you and your daughter that this situation should continue. And who has the power to change lives and to heal? God does, of course. So you grow angry and bitter towards him for allowing these circumstances to continue.

At the same time you remember St. Paul's words, "But who are you, my friend, to talk back to God? A clay pot does not ask the man who made it, 'Why did you make me like this?'" (Rom 9:20). You realize that you can't aim your anger at God, yet you don't know what to do with the emotions that are churning around inside. How do you let this situation act as an opportunity for polishing your prisms rather than for covering them with the dust and grime of resentment?

God Is in Control

First, it helps to remember that this life won't be easy for anyone, including God's children, until he comes in glory. We need to remind ourselves that we are on the way. Our true home is not here on earth but is being prepared for us with the Father. Compared with all eternity, our time on earth is short indeed, even though it may seem that the days drag by. Let us be people who know how to hope, who believe that nothing can separate us from the love of God, and who believe that he can bring glory out of every circumstance, if we but place it in his good hands. A passage from Romans shows that those who have gone before us have encountered the same struggles, which they have overcome by God's grace.

> I consider that what we suffer at this present time cannot be compared at all with the glory that is going to be revealed to us. All of creation waits with eager longing for God to reveal his sons. For creation was condemned to lose its purpose, not of its own will, but because God willed it to be so. Yet there was the hope that creation itself would one day be set free from its slavery to decay and would share the glorious freedom of the children of God. For we know that up to the

> present time all of creation groans with pain, like the pain of childbirth. But it is not just creation alone which groans; we who have the Spirit as the first of God's gifts also groan within ourselves as we wait for God to make us his sons and set our whole being free. For it was by hope that we were saved; but if we see what we hope for then it is not really hope. For who hopes for something he sees? But if we hope for what we do not see, we wait for it with patience.
>
> In the same way the Spirit also comes to us, weak as we are. For we do not know how we ought to pray; the Spirit himself pleads with God for us in groans that words cannot express (Rom 8:18-27).

St. Paul's words offer tremendous encouragement. God's own Spirit intercedes for us with the Father! They also point to a condition that may increase our difficulty. We must remember that we are part of creation and that God is the Creator. Sometimes our pride obscures this fact. Of course we'll be resentful if we fail to accept the fact that life is bound to be difficult at times and that God is the one in control. But our relationship is not just one of creature to creator. God is our Father. And scripture assures us that a good father disciplines the child whom he loves. Though all discipline is unpleasant at the time, it brings the reward of a virtuous life.

If we insist on clinging to resentment, our life will be poisoned from within, just as scripture indicates. But if we give our bitterness to the Lord and repent of pride, Jesus can counter our pain, frustration, and suffering with comfort, mercy, healing, strength, and love. The Father knows and understands how difficult our life is. He sent his only son as an act of love that could be matched only by the son's acceptance of suffering and death for our sake. "Of his own free will he gave up all he had, and took the nature of a servant" (Phil 2:7). God himself, in the person of Jesus, has endured the worst suffering that we can imagine. What a comfort Jesus will be for us if we only let him. Let us be careful not to close off communication with the One Person who can make sense out of our life and bring peace to weary spirits.

Six Steps to Freedom

After we reflect on the temporality of our existence and on the real love that God has for us, there are six remaining steps that will help us to overcome resentment against God.

1. *Ask for the grace to want to be set free.* Unfortunately, something within us prefers to hold a grudge rather than to let go of bitterness. Pray for grace. If you can't bring yourself to pray, reading God's word can restore your spirit so that it desires union with God above all else. Picturing your predicament in terms of the cable blocked by the metal cover might help in these circumstances.

2. *Bring your anger to God's throne.* But don't walk away once you've done that. It may help to say aloud, "Father, I have this awful anger eating at me, and I don't know what to do but to bring it to you. I don't want to hold anything against you, the source of my life. Lead me in your ways, Lord. Let me know deep in my heart that all good things come from you and that only good things come from you. I place my resentment at the foot of your son's cross. Let me keep it there and let it mingle with Jesus' own spirit of forgiveness as he hung on the cross for me. Help me to walk in your ways, O Lord, not in my own poisoned desires."

3. *Meditate on the love and majesty of God.* Reflect on God's love for you. It helps to address the Father out loud, saying things that you know to be true about him, even if you don't particularly "feel" that these are true at the moment. "Father, you are perfect in love and mercy. You have created the whole universe in beautiful harmony, yet you are actively interested in me and my life. You are kind enough to want to polish the prisms of my life, and I thank you for that even though the process hurts. Father, you are far above every other. Help me to love you more."

4. *Ask for the grace to repent of anger and bitterness.*

5. *Express repentance, even when you do not yet experience it in your heart.* "Father, I repent of my anger against you. Please bring me to a place of peace with you. Please work this repentance into my heart. Forgive my pride and stubbornness. Give

me a new heart, O Lord, united to your own loving heart, that I may be set free from this sin. Thank you Lord God."

6. *Ask God to comfort you in the midst of the situation that has caused your resentment.* God's way may not be your way, but his way is always for the good. You can only experience that good, however, when you let God come to you in the middle of your anguish. This holds true even when the event that prompted your bitterness happened years earlier.

As we begin to take these steps toward God, we may not feel humble or repentant or experience God as all love and goodness, but we must begin somewhere. Just making the effort forces us to let go of some of the bitterness. It may take an hour of just crying out to the Lord before we begin to win the victory over bitterness. We may spend our prayer times for the next two weeks covering the same ground, but at least our direction will be right—toward reconciliation with God, not away from him further. And let us remember as we do this that God himself will pray through us, empowering us with his Spirit. "My mind and my body may grow weak, but God is my strength; He is all I ever need" (Ps 73:26).

Resentment against Others

It's one thing to be able to let go of our anger and resentment against God, who is perfect, and another to find the grace to let go of anger and bitterness toward an ordinary, imperfect human being.

The Lord taught me a lesson about this one day while I was mulling over an insult I thought I had received. In my pride, I was growing increasingly bitter about it. I began to read scripture to find solace for my hurt and justification for my anger when I came upon words from Psalm 73: "When my thoughts were bitter and my feelings were hurt, I was as stupid as an animal; I did not understand you" (Ps 73:21-22).

These words shocked me. The psalmist was implying that I was stupid, failing to understand God, when all the while I had been feeling superior in my situation. Wasn't I on God's side, the side of justice? But as I read the psalm and grew to understand God's forgiveness, I saw that I should be humble before him, forgiving others with the help of his grace. In fact, if my pride had been put to death, I would not have been insulted in the first place.

Consider verse 25 of Psalm 73: "Since I have you, what else could I want on earth?" Should we forsake unity with Christ in order to hang on to unforgiveness? Should we lose the pearl of great price in order to get even? It is one thing to forgive people for wrongs that don't particularly bother us, but it's far different to forgive the unforgivable. Yet, that is what Jesus did for us, and that is how he wants us to treat one another. His own words are clear: "If you forgive others the wrongs they have done to you, your Father in heaven will also forgive you. But if you do not forgive others, then your Father will not forgive the wrongs you have done" (Mt 6:14-15).

Fortunately, we are not left on our own to try to work up feelings of forgiveness. The Holy Spirit will give us strength to direct our will to be one with the will of God, and thereby to will to put away bitterness. No doubt we'll suffer setbacks. But God is faithful. Let us relax in the knowledge that he is with us in all our struggles, working in our spirits to give us victory.

Some of us are asked to forgive greater wrongs than others. Perhaps a doctor made a wrong diagnosis of a loved one's illness, which has led to permanent impairment or death. Perhaps someone we loved was killed by a drunk driver. Our husband may have been unfaithful. Our children may be rebellious and disrespectful. It may be that someone has spread lies about us that have ruined our reputation. Perhaps a friend betrayed a confidence. We may not be able to forget the destructive words said in anger, which go to the deepest recesses of our hearts. Forgiveness does not mean that we must become best friends with the drunk driver, the woman who gossips, or the doctor who made a fatal error, but it does mean that we are interested in everyone's salvation. We have put on the mind of Christ and the salvation of others is his most vital interest. Forgiveness means that we will strive to overcome bitterness, which touches our relationships with poison and destroys us in the process.

It's vital to remember that we can't overcome bitterness on our own. We simply are incapable of forgiving the unforgivable. But Jesus isn't. He has taken upon himself the sins of *all* mankind, to set every one of us free. As a result, we, too, are empowered to forgive—to free one another.

Overcoming Bitterness

In dealing with the well of bitterness, let us take each thing before the Lord as he calls it to mind and follow these steps.

1. Ask for the desire to let go of the bitterness.
2. Ask for grace to repent.
3. Meditate on God's character and consider how great is his love for you.
4. Ask for the grace to forgive, remembering that it has been won for you already.
5. Speak words of forgiveness out loud, and for the specific injury. "I forgive my neighbor Joan for ridiculing me in front of others for something I did not do. I do this in your strength and in your love, Jesus."
6. Ask God to make that forgiveness a reality in your life. You will begin to experience victory in your feelings, as well as your will.
7. It may be necessary for restoring a relationship to speak directly with someone who has offended you, to let them know of their offense. It's important to remember that peace and love must inform your motives and goals. The need for this kind of communication is particularly great in close relationships. It would be wrong in a marriage, for example, to spend your time silently forgiving your husband, but never discussing the areas of difficulty that you are pledged to overcome together.
8. Search your conscience to see if you have been responsible, even in part, for the situation that has caused your bitterness. Whenever possible, ask forgiveness directly of the person or people you've wronged. If that's not possible, do so before God.

In some instances where the wrong has been a minor one, you may experience freedom from bitterness immediately. But if your husband has been unfaithful, for example, it may take days to speak of forgiveness out loud, or to desire to overcome bitterness. Don't grow discouraged when this happens. Continue to cry out to the Lord for the grace to let go of your hurts, for the grace to forgive and to be of the same mind as God. Remember, he, too, has experienced betrayal and the wrongful death of loved ones. Insulting words were spoken about him and to him. In all things he has gone before us. He goes before us even now, understanding our hurt, yet urging us to greater holiness, greater unity with him through forgiveness. We shall be able to say with the psalmist: "But as for me, how wonderful to be near God, to find protection with the Lord God and to proclaim all that he has done!" (Ps 73:28).

The Root of Bitterness

Remember Paul's words in his letter to the Hebrews: "Strive for peace with all men, and for the holiness without which no one will see the Lord. See to it that no one fails to obtain the grace of God; that no 'root of bitterness' spring up and cause trouble, and by it the many become defiled" (Heb 12:14-15). Paul speaks of the "root of bitterness." Imagine these roots like those of a dandelion. If you pull up a dandelion but fail to unearth the whole root, the plant will grow back with twice as much foliage.

We can eradicate the root of bitterness by applying the toxin of forgiveness. As it penetrates deeper and deeper, it will dissolve every trace of the root. But we shouldn't try to exterminate the root in just one day. In many cases, it's taken years to grow. We may need to reapply the toxin of forgiveness a number of times. Let us not grow discouraged if a weed sprouts after we thought we had eliminated it. Instead, let us thank God for the opportunity to approach him in humility and confidence, in order to ask for his strength to overcome the temptation to become bitter again.

As you cooperate with God to uproot bitterness in your life, take care that no new root implants itself in you. How should you handle new hurts and difficulties?

1. Ask for the grace to recognize bitterness when you begin to think in resentful ways. Until someone adopts a new way of thinking in Christ, they often fail to recognize these thought patterns as problems.

2. Pray for God's mercy and strength; ask for the grace to forgive or to accept whatever situation you are facing.

3. Renounce bitterness.

4. Get busy with other mind-involving activities, relying on the Lord's strength to work into your heart the act of will that you have just made.

Recognizing the Problem

A good way to recognize bitterness is to realize that it always seeks fertilizer. For example, my husband may forget to say goodbye to me when he leaves for work in the morning. My feelings are hurt. I have two choices. I can simply forgive him—though in this example it's debatable whether he even requires forgiveness—or I can hold his forgetfulness against him. If I choose the latter, I will probably call to mind other examples of my husband's inconsiderateness, thereby adding fertilizer. "He didn't thank me for supper yesterday. Boy, is he getting inconsiderate. He's really taking me for granted." By the time my husband gets home, I will be ready to jump on any little thing that might support my view of him as inconsiderate. If this leads to an argument, as it probably will, there will be even more fertile ground for that root of bitterness to grow.

This small example shows how bitterness always seeks fertilizer. The trick is to stop that root while still a seed. If the wrong done against us is greater than the one in the example, it is doubly important to take time to ask the Lord for the grace to forgive. That way the seed won't have a chance to take root. A forgiving heart and a humble spirit that seeks after God's ways will kill the seeds and roots of bitterness. Remember the words of the psalmist, "When my thoughts were bitter and my feelings were hurt, I did not understand your ways."

Sometimes it may be right to ask forgiveness of one another, but generally, we should not tell another that we forgive them unless they ask for forgiveness. Many people will not use the exact phrase, "I ask your forgiveness for such and such." Instead, they will tell us how awful they feel about something. A simple "I forgive you" in those circumstances can set a person free. Where this is not possible, however, it is tremendously important to have forgiven the person before God. We have discussed this at some length, but I would like to add one more thought for reflection.

Think of someone you love, against whom you are harboring an unforgiving heart. Read these words from the second letter to the Corinthians: "Now, however, you should forgive him and encourage him, in order to keep him from becoming so sad as to give up completely." We really can damage those we love when we refuse to forgive. That's the awful result of our failure to take on God's heart of forgiveness.

But why should we forgive the drunk driver we never met or the doctor who erred? Because God's word is clear. If we do not take on his forgiving heart and leave vengeance to him, we will become like a bitter plant that is poison to ourselves and to everyone we come in contact with. We cut ourselves off from the mercy of God. Our prisms will never reflect the love and glory of God while clouded over with bitterness.

Think of the bitterness that you struggle with most. Is it worth your salvation to hold on to it? I think most of us will answer, "No." By God's power and love, we will choose life. We will go before him humbly, pleading for the grace to let go of our hurt, to forgive the unforgivable, to unite ourselves with forgiveness incarnate on a cross, that his will may be done on earth and his kingdom established. Then will the cloak come off of our lamps and the glow from God's love begin to shimmer through, touching and healing those around us.

FOUR

Fighting Anxiety and Depression

When my oldest son, Matthew, was one-and-a-half, our family moved into a new apartment. Five days later Matthew made another move, this time to the hospital. Sick as he was with pneumonia, Matthew fought hard against the instruments of healing—medication, fluids, food, rest, and the oxygen tent. He must have been very anxious about what was happening to him. He would yell over and over, "I want my Momma!" in spite of the fact that I was holding him at the time. He ignored any toy I brought to cheer him up and comfort him. Nevertheless, his health improved, and at the end of a week's time he was pronounced fit to return home. When I told Matthew that he was going home, I though he would be excited and relieved. Instead he fought getting dressed, screaming and crying to stay. He may have detested the hospital, but at least it was more familiar to him than the home he had lived in for five days. The thought of another change caused him real anxiety, and it wasn't until we were home for many hours and he was surrounded by familiar things and had slept in his own bed that Matthew began to relax and be peaceful again.

Of course my distress through this period was very great. I understood that my son was upset both from the move and the hospitalization. I felt great compassion for his predicament; and my frustration was enormous because I could not hope to make a one-and-a-half-year-old understand why it was good for him to be in the hospital. The only thing I could do was to reassure him with my presence, hoping that he could trust my husband, Russ, and me enough to get through this difficult time.

Matthew recovered from his experience and so did I, and I came away with a much deeper understanding of the Father's love for me and my need to trust him. I could see my own relationship with the Father mirrored in Matthew's relationship with me. Like Matthew, I was often anxious and worried because I refused to accept comfort or solace from anyone. The difficulties I experienced seemed hard and unfair, so I lashed out against my circumstances in order to survive.

Wasn't I just like Matthew? If he could have accepted the fact that I knew more than he did, he might have been able to trust me. We could have had a ball! The hospital had a great playroom, beautiful toys, nice rocking chairs, just made for sick children with their moms. And best of all there was plenty of time to be together. We could have used the time to grow much closer. I was not called away by housework or other errands, and he was not off playing as would have been the case at home. We had uninterrupted time together.

I realized afterwards that I often miss God's blessing because I am worrying about something. I find it difficult to admit that there could be anyone who might know my needs better than I. Instead of trusting myself to the Father and using the time to grow closer to him, I tend to resist the situation.

My predicament is like Matthew's in yet another way. The whole purpose of his stay at the hospital was to heal him. Likewise, the anxious times in my life are times that the Father uses to heal me, often of my sinful ways. If I submit myself to his loving discipline, I will also receive his loving assurance and joy in the midst of my trial. "Come to me, all of you who are tired from carrying heavy loads, and I will give you rest. Take my yoke and put it on you, and learn from me, because I am gentle and humble in spirit; and you will find rest. For the yoke I will give you is easy, and the load I will put on you is light" (Mt 11:28-30). "Can any of you live a bit longer by worrying about it? If you can't manage even such a small thing, why worry about the other things?" (Lk 12:25-26).

"It's a Mother's Right to Worry"

Jesus tells us that it's futile to worry. It changes nothing. Unless we really believe that it's pointless to worry, our attempts to overcome anxiety will be doomed from the outset. We mothers find it particularly difficult to believe that this is true. We often feel that it's our right and responsibility to worry about our children. When we read in scripture that we should give our burdens to the Lord rather than worrying about them, we add mental parentheses: except, of course, mothers who must constantly worry about their children if there is to be any hope for them.

That description used to suit me perfectly. From the moment I found out I was pregnant I would worry about the health and salvation of my children. I was convinced that a good mother worries about her children. The futility of this approach became obvious to me when I was pregnant after having had two children. For some reason, this was the first time I wasn't worried about a miscarriage, even though I had miscarried twice before. I was confident that this baby would be fine. Around the fourth month I began to experience difficulties. My first response was to feel guilty for not having worried! Something told me that if I had only been more worried about the baby, this would not have happened. Though my mind could dismiss such an argument, my heart did not, so I began to worry a great deal. At the same time, I prayed for the baby and asked for the faith to believe in a healing. Even so, I thought that if I could muster up enough faith, I could "earn" the baby's healing. Every day for a month I would go through these mental gymnastics, all the while calling on God for his help. Finally, what should have been perfectly obvious from the start became a reality to me—other than following the doctor's instructions, there was not a single thing I could do to bring that baby to term. It was completely out of my hands. What a relief it was to let go of that burden, to put my child into God's hands alone.

I finally did miscarry, but I was able to accept it, knowing that I was not responsible for maintaining the pregnancy. Even though I didn't understand why God had allowed such a thing, I could approach him humbly, acknowledging his lordship over life and death knowing that his ways are not mine. I was grateful to have nourished for a little time, a life who was now with the Father. Of course, I would miss terribly the joy of those years of nurture after birth. But I was able to receive God's comfort and love. Ironically, the work that God accomplished most dramatically during that difficult time was to help me accept the truth that "His steadfast love endures forever."

An Antidote for Worry

Worry is not the same thing as concern. Proper concern for situations keeps us from acting foolishly. Worry can't prevent a miscarriage, but concern can cause us to obey our doctors' orders. Worrying as our young children cross a street produces no corresponding result in their safety. Concern, however, will cause us to train them to stop, look, and listen before crossing. Worry about how TV affects our children does nothing to alter the situation, but concern will prompt us to monitor their viewing and help set guidelines regarding the quality and quantity of the shows they watch.

Most often, anxiety and worry have a paralyzing effect on us. Feelings of hopelessness entrap and prevent us from determinedly seeking a solution to our difficulties. If we find ourselves trapped in anxiety, we should repent to the Father, admitting our inability and making an act of faith and trust in God's ability to overcome any situation.

Worry is not only ineffectual; it can be harmful. We all know that ulcers and other physical ailments can be caused or aggravated by worry. Worry saps our strength tremendously. No wonder we have trouble putting one foot in front of the other with so many burdens on our shoulders. We need to continue to hand over our burdens to the One whose shoulders are big enough to bear them.

If worry is sapping the strength in your life remember that the antidote is to trust God, to allow him to carry your burdens. If you've been trying to give your burdens to Jesus without much success, ask yourself these questions:

—Do you really believe that you should stop worrying?
—Do you believe that God has your best interests at heart?
—Are you motivated by trust in God and his plan for your life, or are you motivated by the desire for self-preservation? Are you determined that things work out the way you want?

Let's look at the second question. Do you believe that God has your best interests at heart? When we realize who God is, it's hard to believe that we could ever fail to trust him, but most of us do fail at times. Trust takes time, and God is patient. He will lead us step by step. To begin the journey, we can start by entrusting him with areas of our life that are small—a test, a conversation we expect to have later in the day, plans for the weekend, clothes for our families, and so on. Gradually we will learn to entrust more of our lives to God—our children's safety, how we spend our days, our families' salvation, our own salvation. Think of the lengths to which Jesus went to show his love for us. Could we ever doubt for an instant that he loves us?

The third question concerns the desire for self-preservation. It's an obstacle that is closely related to the second. Remember Christ's words: "He who tries to save his life will lose it; but he who loses his life for my sake will have life eternal" (Mt 16:25). It's a natural human tendency to think that we alone know how things should work out in our lives and in the lives of those we love. Our plan probably does not include stress, confrontation, or mistakes. Therefore, in his great love, the Lord will lead us through many situations of stress and many confrontations, allowing us to make many mistakes. He will love us through all these trials, humbling and teaching us that his ways really are better, his plans far more encompassing, and his wisdom far beyond anything that man can imagine.

A time of anxiety can be an opportunity to let go of something or someone, to learn to trust the love of the Father more completely. It is a time for deepening our relationship with the

Lord. These times can strengthen us tremendously. Like my Matthew, we may be afraid of the unknown, but let us dare to trust and take comfort in Jesus.

In Luke 12, after Jesus had admonished the crowd, telling them not to worry, he added "Instead, be concerned with his kingdom, and he will provide you with these things."

An Escape Valve

Anxiety generates a lot of energy. We don't know quite what to do with ourselves. Even when we give the situation to God, through prayer, we can still be left with nervous energy. Sometimes it gets bottled inside, and we sit tight, overcome by the intensity of the burden and afraid that we might explode. This produces the paralyzing effect mentioned earlier. A healthy escape valve can be useful at times like these. Other than scrubbing floors, what, practically speaking, should we do with the energy? The answer is found in Luke 12:31, "Be concerned with his kingdom." Matthew puts it another way: "Happy are those whose greatest desire is to do what God requires; God will satisfy them fully" (Mt 5:6).

When Peter stepped out of the boat to walk on water, he kept his eyes on Jesus; he was doing what the Lord required. As soon as he looked at the wind and the waves and realized that he was doing the impossible, he started to sink. He was worried and anxious. He took his eyes off Jesus and his mind off doing the will of God in that situation. This is a perfect example of what happens to us when we become anxious. Let us learn from Peter's predicament to put our eyes on Jesus, hoping always in him.

After we've prayed, taking our eyes off the difficult situation and placing them on the Lord, we should try to find something practical to do to improve the situation. We need a good outlet for our energy. Perhaps we should write a letter of comfort to a friend experiencing sorrow, draw up a new schedule for ourselves to deal with all the commitments we are having difficulty meeting, call a friend for a list of babysitters if we're having trouble finding one. If our anxiety is caused by someone else's trial, it may be most helpful to intercede regularly for them. That may be the most significant thing we can do for them.

Whatever the situation, we can ask the Lord to show us what we can do to alleviate the problem. Taking this approach will help us to have a much more positive frame of mind. We can go one step further by asking the Lord what he requires of us right then for the sake of his kingdom. We should pray that his will be first in our lives. Sometimes what we should be doing for his kingdom is obvious, such as changing diapers, fixing dinner, folding laundry, writing Christmas cards, picking up the kids from school, going to work, or bringing peace out of the squabble going on in the yard. If that's what God requires, we should want to do these things vigorously, out of love for him, rather than as a formality.

It may help you to make a mental picture. In your hands is a box with whatever is troubling you wrapped up inside. You put it at the foot of the cross, asking the Lord if he would take care of it because it's getting in your way and you don't want to look at it unless he's present. After that you can go about his business with much more freedom. If it starts bothering you again, you've taken the box back. You simply need to return it to Jesus right away.

Sometimes it's hard to know what God requires of us. At those times we must seek for direction through prayer, scripture, and perhaps the help of another Christian. If we are married, we can ask our husbands for advice. Whatever we do should be done out of love, since God is calling us to love and unity with himself and our brothers and sisters.

If we wake up feeling unable to face the day, uncertain of how we will get through it in one piece, we might try thinking about only the next fifteen minutes of it. We may not feel up to handling a whole day's worries, but surely we can put them aside for the next few minutes as we make the beds. When fifteen minutes are over, we can ask the Lord for strength to tackle the next job, perhaps the dishes—a twenty-minute chore. As we go through the day in this manner, we will discover two things: we can do what seems impossible with the help of our enabling God; and our day can be productive even though we think we only have energy to worry. Many facets of our lives have been strengthened as a result. We have not just survived; we have overcome.

It may take practice before we learn to make good use of this technique. No doubt, the effort required from us will be great. But the results are well worth the energy expended. None of us can go through this life without troubles. To carry on effectively, we've got to approach our difficulties with faith.

What about Depression?

If we remain anxious for too long, we will begin to sink into depression. Nothing can sap our strength the way depression does, and most of us simply cannot afford to waste time being depressed. I'm not talking about legitimate sorrow, or occasional touchy days. I am talking about the kind of depression that sneaks up on us, trying to catch us unawares, leaving us caught in a whirlpool that we feel helpless to escape from.

Of course some depression has physical causes and some is so serious that the individual cannot function without counselling and medication. But I'm talking about the kind of depression that nearly everyone experiences once in a while. We may feel anxious without knowing why. Perhaps we have a hard time sleeping. We may find ourselves becoming helpless and then hopeless; pretty soon nothing can cheer us up. We don't like feeling this way but feel powerless to stop. Often self-pity is at work in the midst of this cycle. We may feel victimized by circumstances or by other people; we may direct our self-pity inward in the form of self-loathing. Why can't we at least *seem* to function "normally" as does everyone else we know?

Sometimes this state of depression can result from periods of boredom. We may be busy enough but think that something more exciting or significant should be happening. If we lack mountains to climb and worlds to conquer, we can grow impatient with our lot and our life. Unable to understand what's happening, we may become anxious because we don't seem to be growing as we think we should. At this point it's very easy to begin feeling depressed. Once again the antidote is to seek first the kingdom of God. As we go before the Lord daily in prayer, seeking his will for our lives, we may find that we need to accept the fact that this is a season when God is working quietly within us. This kind of season can have a tremendous effect on our relationship with God. If we are faithful in little things, then the Father will entrust us with greater tasks. Even if our entire life is spent in quiet and undramatic pursuits, our prisms can truly reflect the glory of the Father as long as we remain faithful and united to him. In fact most of us are called to a quiet life. Very few of us lead "spectacular" lives, and those who do must face the same struggles as the rest of us. They probably cherish greatly the ordinary things of their lives. The only way to live, whatever our lot, is to be open to the will of the Father and grateful to him for the lot he has given us.

Overcoming Depression

If we have already begun the descent to depression, we may need more help. I used to think of depression as a whirlpool. Its unlucky victims were caught in it with no chance of escape. That view was mistaken. I've come to understand that depression is much more like a spiral staircase. We start down slowly, but as we go further, momentum builds until it seems that we are being pushed along. The lower we go, the harder it is to turn around and climb back. It takes tremendous strength to even consider such a thing. But with God's help, that strength can be ours. If we begin to look around for help on our journey downward, we will notice doorways at different intervals on several levels. Some of these will lead to other routes back to the top, perhaps gradual slopes that are easier to walk than climbing the stairs. Behind other doors may be people who are waiting to help us along, providing walking sticks and strong arms to support us. Occasionally we will find an elevator behind the doors and the Lord, himself, at the controls, waiting to give us an express ride up.

When viewed in this way, depression appears as it truly is—

something that we can overcome by God's grace. Along with depression come feelings of helplessness and hopelessness that can make it tremendously difficult for us to even look for a door. Therefore, the first step is to tell someone that we are depressed and in need of prayer. Real strength comes from the prayers of others. We can rely on their strength in the Lord to help us to open one of the doors.

Reading scripture, particularly the psalms, can also strengthen us to open a door. God's word nourishes and strengthens the life of the Spirit within us. It can give us courage and hope to pray for greater strength. Whenever possible, we should pray out loud so that the words of our prayer will become more of a reality to us. We may not "feel" the words but we can "will" them:

> Lord God, I thank you that you have come among us to be our Savior. I thank you for the gift of your Spirit. Your ways are good and holy, perfect beyond measure. I want to be your servant, Lord. I desire to be a strong and holy woman for your sake. I ask that you strengthen my will to do what is right and pleasing in your sight. Strengthen my will to fight this depression. In your name, Jesus, I stand firm against this depression. I want no part of it. Remove it and replace it with your joy. I repent of any self-pity or cowardice that would weaken me and my service to you. I desire strength and not weakness, even if you will require great service from me. I am happy to do your will. Come to me, Lord. Show me the way out. Help me accept whatever vehicle you may offer to bring me out of this depression. I follow you, Jesus. Lead me out of this trap. You are the God of miracles. You can do all things, and so it is in confidence that I come before you now. Thank you, Lord God.

God is eager to answer such a prayer. When we have the courage to pray, our hearts open up to the Lord's strength and peace.

Music can also help us keep our eyes on Jesus. It can even take great effort at times to put on a Christian record. When someone feels depressed, every action takes great deliberation and strength. But with the help of our enabling God, we can put on a record that will remind us that God is with us. He is greater than us, greater than our enemy, greater than our depression. Sometimes we can even force ourselves to sing. As we begin to act in a more joyful and positive manner, we will see that we are indeed strong in Christ. We will know that we can be rid of this depression. We may not succeed at this at first, but if we persist we will become more and more successful.

Whenever possible, we can ask brothers and sisters to pray with us. If we know another Christian who can advise us, we can ask for specific advice and decide in advance to follow it. If we are married, we can ask our husbands for help. God has always used my husband in this way, even though his advice wasn't always what I wanted to hear. Sometimes he talked with me, prayed with me, took me out for an evening, sent me to bed for more sleep, or told me to snap out of it and do the work at hand. Sometimes his advice was hard to follow, but it always led toward my release from depression, sometimes instantly, sometimes by starting me on the way back up. If I had rebelled against Russ' advice, I would have missed God's blessing for my life.

Wives must be particularly careful not to use depression as a tool to manipulate their husbands. Often unconsciously, we use anxiety or depression as an emotional weapon to get attention or to get our own way. Singles, too, can manipulate their friends or roommates in similar ways. Manipulation is certainly not the quality of a strong, valiant woman, and if we are guilty of this, we need to be quick to repent. If we're guilty of this kind of behavior, we should take extra precautions to guard against it.

Sometimes we may not know why we are depressed or moody. We may have great difficulty working out of it. Sometimes, simply deciding not to be depressed but to proceed with life as usual will free us from depression. This may sound too simple, but I have known many instances when it has worked when all else has failed.

Moodiness is always an obstacle to loving others. If we indulge our moods, we are placing ourselves first. But if we put the temptations to moodiness aside, we will be able to put the Father's will first, and we will be able to reach out to our brothers and sisters as well. We've all known people whose emotions are steady. What a blessing it is to know that our relationship with them does not depend on how they're feeling at the moment.

Whatever your situation or reason for becoming depressed, God has a way out. There will be doors provided for you, if you dare to look for them. May you have strength and courage in Christ to open the door and find the way up.

> The Lord says to his people, "When the time comes to save you, I will show you favor and answer your cries for help. I will guard and protect you and through you make a covenant with all peoples. I will let you settle once again in your land that is now laid waste. I will say to the prisoners, 'Go free!' and to those who are in darkness, 'Come out to the light!' They will be like sheep that graze on the hills; they will never be hungry or thirsty. Sun and desert heat will not hurt them, for they will be led by one who loves them. He will lead them to springs of water. I will make a highway across the mountains and prepare a road for my people to travel. My people will come from far away, from the north and the west, and from Aswan in the south." Sing, heavens! Shout for joy, earth! Let the mountains burst into song! The Lord will comfort his people; he will have pity on his suffering people (Is 49:8-13).

The Lord's promises are true and we can rely on him. We can respond to him by "coming out to the Light." Our prisms will dazzle brilliantly as we rely on Jesus, as we become strengthened in his ways, allowing him to polish and purify our lives.

FIVE

Love Is Never Irritable

One of the most famous and stirring passages of scripture is found in Paul's first letter to the Corinthians. It's the famous love chapter.

> I may be able to speak the languages of men and even of angels, but if I have no love, my speech is no more than a noisy gong or a clanging bell. I may have the gift of inspired preaching; I may have all knowledge and understand all secrets; I may have all the faith needed to move mountains—but if I have no love, I am nothing. I may give away everything I have, and even give up my body to be burned—but if I have no love, this does me no good.
> Love is patient and kind; it is not jealous or conceited or proud; love is not ill-mannered or selfish or irritable; love does not keep a record of wrongs; love is not happy with evil, but is happy with the truth. Love never gives up; and its faith, hope, and patience never fail (1 Cor 13:1-5).

When I was a child, this passage never failed to inspire me. But as I grew older, my response was mixed. These words were inspiring. But I found it so difficult to live up to them. I became very discouraged, almost losing hope that I could ever love with the kind of pure love that Paul talks about. Such perfection was reserved for the great saints. I was tempted to become angry at Paul for advocating such an impossible ideal.

How could love never be irritable? This statement frustrated me more than anything. Though I seemed like a serene individual, irritation was usually my first reaction to anything unpleasant. And it took great effort to prevent my irritability from showing. It was such an instinctive reaction that I felt defeated in every attempt to overcome it. Even so I managed to pray once or twice that God would take away my problem with irritability. This one fault contributed more than any other to my feeling a failure as a Christian.

Fortunately, God hears even our feeblest prayers. Though I still have much to learn, God has helped me to overcome my problem with irritability. And he did it without my realizing it. As I put other areas of my life under his lordship, the irritability I felt began to disappear. In fact, I've found that it is best to deal with other areas of my life first, rather than attacking irritability head on.

Feeling and Acting

It is one thing to feel irritable and another to act irritably. It's not a sin to feel irritable as your first response to a situation. But to cater to the irritable feelings by thinking in ways that allow the irritability to build up until it results in gossip or slander is plainly wrong. We can master our mind, tongue, tone of voice, and body movements so that we respond appropriately to the situation. So, you see, it's difficult to attack feelings of irritability but possible and helpful to directly attack the irritable action.

Irritation shouldn't be confused with righteous anger in the face of injustice. Anger can be an appropriate response in a given situation. But Paul says, "Love is never irritable." Often it's enough simply to control our response in the right way at the first sign of irritability. We can decide not to act irritably despite the fact that we feel irritable. That may be all that's necessary to free us from the feelings. So the irritated response or action can and should be controlled directly and actively by us. But feelings of irritability will usually need to be attacked on other fronts. We will need to discover why we become irritated so easily.

No Pedestals Please

Freedom from irritability is not an impossible goal. As I mentioned, I was tempted to think that the ideal that Paul held up in Corinthians was limited to the kind of people that my husband calls the "big guns" of the Christian life. But when I thought about the chapter that preceeded Paul's description of love—reminding us that we are all members of one body—I could see that this kind of thinking was the opposite of Paul's intention. We can fall into the habit of thinking of God's word as something possible for some people to fulfill but impossible for others. We tend to put people on pedestals. They're the holy ones, the great saints, not us. Most of us have a set of these "holy people" in our lives. They may be Christians who lead prayer meetings, who teach and preach. We may put other women on a pedestal who are always helping others, who are involved in many aspects of church life. They always know the right thing to say and do. We may feel dwarfed by them in comparison (there we go making comparisons again). Of course, it's good to have someone to look up to, but it's a mistake to write off our own responsibility to strive after perfection on the theory that we could never be good enough, could never be like one of the people we've placed on the pedestal.

In his first letter to the Corinthians, Paul addressed this very problem. Chapter 12 talks about the unity and diversity of the body, in which each person has an important part. One part is not greater than another, but each is unique and all are interdependent. At the end of that chapter Paul talks about the more visible or spectacular gifts like healing, working miracles, and talking in strange tongues, emphasizing the fact that not all will receive these gifts. He goes on to say, "Set your hearts, then, on the more important gifts. Best of all, however, is the following way" (1 Cor 12:31).

The following way is described in the next chapter of Corinthians, the chapter on love, which we have already discussed. How is it possible for us to set our hearts on such a high ideal? To do so, Paul tells us that we must give up being a child and agree to grow up for the sake of the kingdom. "When I was a child, my speech, feelings, and thinking were all those of a child; now that I am a man, I have no more use for childish ways" (1 Cor 13:11). And this way, Paul says, is open to us all.

Self-Condemnation

Whether we are 21 or 71 God is calling us to give up childish ways so that we might grow up in him. If we are older, we should fight the temptation to condemn ourselves, thinking that we should be farther along than we are. God has his hand on us now. That is what counts. He will use everything that has gone on before this moment and turn it to glory as only he knows how. Most of us are probably in much better shape than we think, anyway. The most essential point is that we are loved by Jesus. This is the place to begin and end. God is on our side, encouraging and guiding us. We need only trust him enough to let him lead us.

It may sound frightening to renounce your childish ways. After all, they may not be good ways, but you are used to them. Take the step anyway. Rebuke your fears, telling them that Jesus is bigger than they are. Remember that Jesus is your strength. Then say aloud to the Lord: "Jesus, I want to do your will. I want to grow up to be the person you want me to be. I will give up my own childish ways. Teach me, Lord, and lead me on the path to your kingdom."

Let us be careful to keep our eyes on Jesus and not on the progress of others as we begin giving up our childish ways. It is tempting but wrong to postpone our own growth because someone else has not yet outgrown their childish ways. When God calls us, let us be bold enough to run forward, saying "amen" to all that he wants to do in and for us. And let us remember Paul's words, "We know that in all things God works for good with those who love him, those whom he has called according to his purpose" (Rom 8:28).

Love in Action

The same is true for irritability. Irritation can serve as a test of how well we are loving others. Remember, irritation can be an indication that another area of our lives needs help. We can put our feeling of irritation to good use by discovering why such a reaction was evoked in us. The way we live out the details of our days is a measure of the way we are loving others.

A children's program called "Mr. Roger's Neighborhood" offers this practical view of love in a song: "There are many ways to say I love you. There's the working way, the sleeping way, the cooking way, the cleaning way, the playing way, the hugging way." The song tries to help children understand that their parents are loving them even when they are doing something other than expressing outright affection for them. In a similar way, I know that my family can experience my love for them by everything I do and say, even when they are not with me as I perform certain tasks. When all the clothes are cleaned and put into drawers, my family experiences my love for them. And when some of the children become old enough to do chores themselves, my patient, non-hysterical reminders of their responsibility for their tasks will also help them see my love for them.

An Irritability Checklist

My day and how I spend it are important to God and to my family. So when irritation begins to mount, I should make a mental checklist of possible causes for it. Such a list can help me sort through my day and my feelings; it can help me tackle the root problems.

Here are some things to check off first.

1. Are you overtired? If you always stay up too late, it's probably time to change that habit.
2. Are you premenstrual? Of course, you can't change that habit, but it can help to know that your period is near. It can

remind you that your perspective may be getting a little off center.

3. Are you pregnant? If you're like me you will hardly ever feel rested when you're pregnant. Chances are that your hormones will have a big effect on your emotional life.
4. Are you approaching menopause? Even before physical symptoms appear, your hormones may be changing. You will need to make some adjustments because of this.
5. Do you need a physical checkup? If your health seems to have been deteriorating lately, perhaps a physical examination is in order.
6. Have you been under a great deal of strain? If so, it can account for your irritability, even though it doesn't excuse you for *acting* irritably. It may help to talk to someone about the strain you've been experiencing.
7. Is your schedule too full? Do you have too much to do in too little time? If so, why not sit down and work out a schedule that is more reasonable? Your husband may be able to help you sort through your priorities.
8. Are you rebelling against your lot in life? If so, repent and trust in the Lord.
9. Are you expecting perfection from yourself or from those around you? Remember the importance of being ready to train others or to forbear their faults, whichever is most appropriate to a situation. If you are expecting too much, remember to repent of any impatience that you've shown to yourself or another.

Apart from physical considerations, then, you may need to work on other areas of your life. For instance, if you're always running out the door, arriving at your destination out of breath and several minutes late, having forgotten something you meant to bring along, perhaps you've got too many activities going at once. It might be wise to consider dropping some of them, or you may need to learn to be more efficient. It takes time to make out a schedule, but it's worth it. It can take the pressure off so that things get done more peacefully. It's usually also a good idea to prepare things ahead of time so that everything will not have to be done at the last minute (usually before the kids leave for school).

This might mean changing some of our ways, but didn't we pray, "Jesus, your ways, not mine?" I don't like preparing lunches the night before, but whenever I do, the next day always goes better because it gets off to a good start. Little changes can make a big difference for our lives. If we have trouble thinking clearly in the early morning it can help to lay out our clothes the night before and to train our children to do the same. This kind of simple preparation can save us lots of frustration the next morning.

Mismatched Expectations

Another common source of irritation comes from mismatched expectations. Perhaps you've been preparing a checklist of all the jobs that need to get done (with your husband's help) over the weekend. These jobs may seem so obvious and pressing to you that you assume your husband anticipates them, too. After all, he has eyes. Saturday comes, however, and he surprises the children with tickets for the doubleheader that day. You react by becoming irritated or angry, even though you've been wanting the children and their dad to do something like this for a long time. You may even begin to feel guilty for being so irritated. It helps to realize that the whole episode is simply a case of mismatched expectations, caused by a lack of communication.

Sometimes mismatched expectations occur because we're afraid to mention something that our husbands might disagree with. We think that if we pop it as a surprise and catch him off guard he may see things our way.

At other times we may simply have misunderstood something someone has said to us. For instance, if a friend says, "Let's have lunch together on Thursday," you may assume that you are going to a restaurant. However, when you arrive at her house to pick her up, you find that she has prepared a lunch for the two of you. You become irritated even though the main purpose of your lunch was simply to spend time together. You had been looking forward to eating out. But your friend hadn't realized when you told her, "I'll be by at 12:15," that you meant you would be picking her up, not staying.

The best way to counteract mismatched expectations is to talk and to listen. We must be willing to change our minds and our plans, to put another's wishes ahead of ours, to realize that we will not always get our own way. In short, we must be willing to grow up. We can trust that God will see to it that our needs will be met. Of course it's important to articulate our needs to those in a position to take care of them. But once we have done that, we should feel grateful if the opportunity presents itself to provide for someone else's needs. I have often thought that I knew my needs exactly. I was the best judge of how to get them taken care of. Yet as I was called to give up my own need (to give up my childish ways) for the sake of someone else's need, I have found that God takes care of me in a much better way than I ever could. Growing up means dying to self, giving up our own ways. This is the lesson that will ultimately enrich our lives and strengthen our families. But remember, we must do these things out of love and gratitude to God, who poured out his life for us. Otherwise we run the risk of becoming bitter or manipulative women, who are decidedly unhappy.

Accepting Daily Frustrations

At one point I found myself becoming irritated at everything, from the spilled milk to junk mail. As I prayed about the problem, I discovered that I simply was not accepting my lot in life. My idea of life did not correspond at all to what was actually happening.

As I planned my days, I planned for my ideal, not for the reality that was around me. Reality consisted of an oven that did not work, a washing machine that was always on the blink, bad weather, and a house that got itself dirty faster than I could get it clean. Naturally I had planned all sorts of "interesting" activities that did not take the hard facts of life into account. As a result, I became frustrated about everything. I could not enjoy my fun projects, knowing that basic order in the house was breaking down. Yet, I didn't enjoy the work at hand because I wanted to be doing something else, accomplishing some other task. Trying to do both things at once simply made matters worse. I needed to accept my lot. Instead of buying food for the oven in the hope that it would be fixed that week, I began to plan my meals around the stove and skillet. I worked on a schedule to clean my house, knowing that it would take time before I could do any more little projects. I developed alternative plans for doing laundry in case the washer broke down.

Since this was my life, I wanted to enjoy it. Why make life miserable for the next twenty years? I repented that I had tried to make my life something other than the Lord wanted it to be. I accepted his forgiveness, asked for his mercy, strength, and grace, and then began to enjoy my life in a way that I hadn't in the past. It took effort, but God gave me new joy through it all. I even began to have time for some of those projects I had never felt quite peaceful pursuing. And much of my irritability vanished.

So through the experience of feeling irritated with all the little things that were going wrong, God opened up a big area of my life to his grace. Once I accepted the fact that spilled milk, mechanical breakdowns, and junk mail were just part of life, they lost their ability to irritate.

Complaining

A complaining attitude breeds irritability. Remember the two thieves that hung on crosses next to Jesus. One was very bitter, asking Jesus why he didn't simply get down from the cross if he had the power to. The other thief simply asked for mercy, knowing that he was getting what he deserved. Don't we resemble the first thief at times? We complain about our circumstances in the same way that the unrepentant thief did: "If you are God why don't you do something about this situation? Can't you see I'm hurting?"

The Father knows how we hurt; that's why he sent Jesus.

And Jesus himself underwent tremendous suffering, but he didn't get down from the cross, undeserving though he was of such treatment. Neither did he save the life of the good thief, though he promised him eternal life. Jesus will not always remove our difficulties either. But we do have the comfort that he has gone before us in all things. He has promised not to make our cross heavier than we can bear with his help. Of course if we try to carry our crosses by ourselves we'll fall flat on our faces. Sometimes I get so used to carrying it with the help of the Holy Spirit that I begin to think that I'm doing most of the work. And I seem to be doing a pretty good job of it, too. But God, in his great mercy, removes his help for a time and let's me fall on my face again. Then I'm in a much better position to repent and to ask for God's strength with renewed humility. For what can any creature do for his creator that the creator could not do for himself? It is only through God's unimaginable love that we even exist; yet we dare to go before him, demanding to know why he allows us to carry a cross!

So a complaining attitude will surely make us irritable. Such pride can best be dealt with by repentance and by meditating thankfully on the greatness and kindness of our God.

Problem Relationships

Sometimes our irritation at the actions of others is triggered by the kind of behavior that we recognize and dislike in ourselves. We have done our best to ignore our problem, rather than to repent and ask for the Lord's help with it. To deal with that source of irritation we need to pray that the Lord will give us his love for the other person. We should reflect on the mercy that Jesus has shown us. Once we do that, we'll be able to repent and ask for God's grace in overcoming the behavior that we dislike in ourselves.

Sometimes we can become irritated at another's weakness. We may even feel some pride that we don't share that weakness. When we realize that such pride is probably worse than the disturbing behavior, we should become humble and repentant for our pride. Such humility will enable us to "forbear with one another out of love" (Eph 4:2) and to "account all others as better" (Phil 2:3). Forbearance is so important in family life. We must be wise and gentle in our loving. Real love has the kind of strength that no amount of assertiveness training can duplicate.

We can't expect people to change overnight simply because we have overcome one or two temptations to act nasty. We will need the grace to endure. We should pray faithfully that God will transform our attitudes toward someone we are having difficulty loving, that he will give us his own love, forbearance, and mercy. We should also pray sincerely for the other person, that God's glory be made more manifest in their lives. We should guard against the temptation to pray for the other so that our own life may become easier. Many saints have gone out of their way to spend time with people they found it difficult to love. They knew that by doing this they would have the opportunity to grow in love, humility, and endurance. They, like us, decided to give up their childish ways.

Peace and Not Disaster

Another common cause of irritability stems from thinking that any misunderstanding is the beginning of the end. You might have a minor misunderstanding with your husband at 7 a.m. and be convinced by 9 a.m. that your marriage is on the rocks—all the joy has slipped away. I used to think I was the only one who felt that way until I started talking to other women. In fact it commonly happens that a whole plan of disaster unfolds before us whenever something goes wrong.

Imagine the following scenario. You all wake up late one morning, your husband, yourself, and the children. You rush around, growing more tense and irritated in the process. The bathrooms are in use, homework cannot be located, and breakfast consists only of juice and a roll—no time for coffee. Normally your husband takes one child to school while you take the other to the babysitter. But as he runs out the door he exclaims, "I'm sorry, but I just can't take him today. If I miss this meeting, it could mean my job!"

"Well, what about mine?" you mutter as you gather the children together.

You drop each child off and go on to work still upset from the morning's rush. You arrive barely on time and plunge immediately into the day's work. But at 9:15, as you sit down for your coffee break (and your first cup of coffee for the day), you think back over the morning with growing weariness. You picture a long procession of mornings that grow worse each day. You imagine that things will get so bad that by the end of next week your husband will refuse to take responsibility for dropping your son off at school. You're sure that he will find ways to eliminate other chores as well, with the result being more work and fatigue for you. The morning's irritations have degenerated into thoughts of a bleak future accompanied by the seeds of bitterness and self-pity.

A way to counteract this imagined plan of disaster and the accompanying negative emotions is to get on top of those thoughts with the truth.

> It is true that we had a misunderstanding this morning. But it will get worked out. We love each other. Our marriage isn't perfect, but it is a very good one. There's no reason to think that he wants our relationship to be like it was this morning any more than I want it to. Jesus, help me accept the truth. I pray for my husband and myself today. Use this incident to bring good fruit into our lives. I ask you to bless my husband's day and to bless mine. Keep me in the center of your will. Help me to see my faults and to repent. And give me the grace to forgive my husband for anything he may have done wrong this morning. Thank you, Jesus.

If you become worried again during the day, you can simply renounce the worry and quickly offer your life to the Lord once again. God doesn't want any of us to be disaster-prone. Our crosses are heavy enough without borrowing ones that haven't been given us.

Expect to Correct

Some situations might justly call for anger as a response, and we should not confuse such anger with unwarranted irritability. If our children are being unkind, we should be angry and should correct them. That doesn't mean that we should expect our children to be perfect or that we should become angry with them every time they do something wrong. We should expect the way we train them to bear fruit in their lives. But if as an adult I still need to repent and be forgiven for wrongdoing, I shouldn't be surprised to find that a child of only two, five, or ten years is not yet perfect.

Therefore, I should emblazon on my mind the words *expect to correct*. This is my duty before God. If I realize this, I won't be surprised, unprepared, or irritated to find that the children require discipline. It's my responsibility to continually train my children in the way that God asks of me. It is also my joy to surround my children with affection, and since I am not irritated with them it is much easier to do this. I enjoy my children tremendously, and we have great affection for each other, but I do not expect as a result of this relationship that they will be perfect. Learning that I should expect to correct my children cleared up more of my irritability than any other single thing (except, perhaps, learning to submit to my husband).

Husband and Wife

I won't describe the role of husband and wife here in detail because I feel it is better treated as a separate subject. Though it's God's plan for us to submit to our husbands, the desire to control our lives is deep, and dying to self comes hard to us all. Yet, if we have the wrong attitude toward our husbands, we will be irritated by almost everything they do. We may think that we're simply "incompatible." But, too often, incompatibility is just another word for selfishness on the part of one or both parties. The pride involved in this kind of irritation is so hurtful.

If you recognize this pride in yourself, consider again who

you are in relation to God. It has been said that God's act of creating and loving us, giving us a share in his kingdom, could be compared to us inviting a chicken to become one of our family. We certainly are not worthy of the great outpouring of love that Jesus has extended to us. Yet we dare to judge a brother or sister as if we were better or more worthy than they. Imagine being irritated with Jesus for the way he hung up clothes or washed dishes or parked the car! Imagine how crushed we would be if we thought that every time we did something he was disdainful or irritated at us. How sad life would be. Let us beg God's mercy and love, especially if we have reached the end of our own ability to love or be merciful. Let us offer our husbands the honor and love we should give to every child of the living God.

Combatting Irritability

In summary, I would offer these suggestions for combatting irritability.

1. Ask yourself why something irritates you. When you discover why, look for a solution to the difficulty.
2. Offer your day to the Lord early in the morning. Seek to be in the center of his will and ask for grace to be a strong and holy woman, to "give up childish ways."
3. Call friends that can encourage you. You needn't always supply details. It's usually enough to simply say, "Pray for me."
4. Call on the Lord: "Help me. Deliver me. Purify me for your name's sake."

One reason I like thinking about women as prism lamps is because of the particular blend of qualities that characterize such a lamp. It is artfully solid. The colors reflected off of the prisms are always gentle shades, ever-changing, combining and shimmering in the light. The lamp is also of great usefulness, but manages to provide its service with real grace and beauty.

I, too, would like to be solid and sure, but with grace, beauty, and gentleness. All too often, I feel like a bare lightbulb hanging in the middle of the ceiling. True, I am being useful. But can't my light be more gentle, less harsh and ugly? Jesus reached out, showing me a new way, polishing off my prisms, and providing the solid base upon which I can rest my life. May he do the same for each of you.

SIX

Defeating Discouragement

Scripture tells us that love and joy ought to characterize our lives as Christians. But why is it that discouragement often swallows up the love and joy? There are many causes for discouragement, but one that operates frequently is the one I call the Holy Saturday Syndrome. This kind of discouragement often occurs after we've engaged in a time of real spiritual battle. We have managed to remain faithful to the Lord through a time of sorrow or suffering, because God has poured out his grace on us. This happens especially in the face of major temptation. By God's grace we have either managed to hold our ground, or we have repented and returned to him if we have slipped a little. It's been a Good Friday experience for us.

Having passed through this time of trial successfully, we expect resurrection joy and power to begin operating in our lives. We usually do not expect to be confronted with Holy Saturday. Imagine what the Saturday after Jesus' death must have been like for the disciples. They had lived through Friday with him, and it was now the Sabbath, a day set aside for glorifying God. But the disciples must have known only fear and loss and waiting. Here was the Messiah, in whom they had placed all their hopes, dead in a tomb. Talk about discouragement! They must have experienced the kind of letdown that happens to a person once the adrenaline stops flowing after a highly emotional experience. All of a sudden, it's back to business as usual. Certainly there must have been many occasions when they needed to encourage one another with the words from Psalm 37: "Be patient and wait for the Lord to act; don't be worried about those who prosper or those who succeed in their evil plans. Don't give in to worry or anger; it only leads to trouble. Those who trust in the Lord will possess the land, but the wicked will be driven out" (7-9).

Sunday morning probably didn't appear much brighter to them. In fact, we read in John's gospel that Mary, when she discovered the empty tomb, was distraught to think that Jesus' body had been snatched away. In Mark's gospel, Mary runs to the disciples to tell them that she has seen Jesus alive. They were "mourning and crying and when they heard her say that Jesus was alive and that she had seen him, they did not believe her" (Mk 16:10-11). Aren't we just like that? We get so wrapped up in discouragement, self-pity, and our own suffering that we don't believe the resurrection reports that we hear. Neither did the apostles believe. They even rejected the evidence of the two travellers to Emmaus. Scripture says, "Last of all, Jesus appeared to the eleven disciples as they were eating. He scolded them, because they did not have faith and because they were too stubborn to believe those who had seen him alive (Mk 16:14). He then addressed to them the great commission to go and preach the good news to the ends of the earth.

Be Quick to Repent and Receive Forgiveness

Fortunately, the apostles did not remain discouraged. They needed to be rebuked by Jesus. After all, they would not have been discouraged had they believed the word that was told them and acted on it. As always they needed to be quick to repent and to receive forgiveness, so that they could go on with the work that Jesus gave them. And we must do the same. If we are experiencing a season of discouragement and are blaming God for it, we may need to repent for failing to believe and act on his word.

The book of Haggai has something to say about waiting for victory and believing the word spoken to us. After returning from captivity in Babylon, the people of Israel were only concerned with building their own homes and businesses, while the Temple lay in ruins. The prophet Haggai called them to repentance, and the entire nation began to rebuild the Temple. Their time of blessing did not begin when they repented, however. Nor did it begin when they started to haul the lumber and cut the massive stones. Instead, we read, "Today is . . . the day that the foundation of the Temple has been completed. See what is going to happen from now on. Although there is no grain left, and the grapevines, fig trees, pomegranates, and olive trees have not yet produced, yet from now on I will bless you" (Hg 2:18). When God's people had put all their energy into their own concerns, "the working man could not earn enough to live on." But once they expended energy and resources to honor God, then the time of blessing came. But not immediately. First the Lord needed to witness the fruit of their repentance.

It's like that for us, too. But even though I know that's true, I still grow impatient for Easter. the apostles, I have experienced Easters before and know that Jesus has won the victory for me, for all time. As Christians, we have good reason to be patient as we wait for the Lord. Haven't we been given the Holy Spirit to be with us always? After a time of Good Friday in our lives it may sometimes please the Lord to have us live out a Saturday experience. Unlike the apostles, we can keep our eyes on the victory that is already won. We may be tempted to look back, give in to discouragement, or slip into self-pity, but let's keep our eyes on Jesus. For he is our victory and our blessing. He is our prize, our pearl of great price, and we are a blessed people indeed.

Faith: Our Guide through the Maze

Another way to understand discouragement is to imagine a maze. In the middle of a season of discouragement it may seem as though we're making no progress at all; we just keep bumping our heads against a wall. We may fear that we'll never make our way out of the present situation or that we've already become hopelessly lost on our way to the Father's house. If we think of this season of discouragement in terms of a maze, we will see that it has a beginning and an end. We'll realize that we can't go too far astray because a maze has only one entrance and one exit. As long as we are determined to follow the voice of the Lord, we can be assured that he will lead us gently along the path.

I like to picture myself putting up markers in case I ever find myself travelling these paths again. If I have tried one direction and run against a brick wall, I can put up a sign, "This didn't work." Every time I successfully turn a corner, I put up an arrow to indicate that I'm on the right path. Even if I do not have to go through this maze again, such mental signposts can enable me to help others who are working their way through.

In the midst of discouragement we are tempted to grow weary, but let us not lose heart. Instead, let us strive to be in the center of God's will, firm in the knowledge that he can turn our mourning into joy. Let us wait upon his voice and his time for moving on. Let us look to the scriptures and diligently work to obey his word, which was brought to us and bought for us with such love. It would be a great disaster were we to turn in rebellion and smash our way out of the maze, leaving ourselves unprotected and far from the Shepherd whose voice we need to hear.

What about the times when you long to follow the Shepherd but don't seem to hear his voice? First, try to get direction by reading and studying scripture. Second, consult a mature Christian who can offer sound guidance. If you are married, seek advice from your husband. Third, make your prayer one with the words of the psalmist: "Cleanse me of my unknown faults, O Lord." Trust your life and your salvation to the risen Lord.

Consider the Magi. They were following the star, working their way through the maze, if you will. What happened when they lost sight of it? They continued in the same general direction and sought help from the source they thought the most reliable. Setting out from Herod's, they saw the star again and rejoiced. Clearly, they had to seek help before finding the right track. But instead of returning by way of Herod, they took a different route home. Why? Because God touched their lives in a direct and powerful way and spoke to them in a dream, giving them new direction. We can trust that God will do the same for us. If we are determined to follow the Lord's will for our lives, he will be there to protect and guide us.

Whose Burdens?

I'd like to return to the maze now. Imagine that a large pool of sparkling water stands before the entrance. Before going in, we must shed all the packages we're carrying in order to be washed and refreshed in the water. Feeling invigorated we pick up our packages and enter the maze full of strength and confidence. Later, we become discouraged when the way seems long and hot and our packages begin to feel like burdens. In fact, we find that we have to discard some of them because the pathways have smaller and smaller entrances. But we like carrying things and find it difficult to let go of them. We may even pick up packages that others have left behind, thinking that they will prove useful later on. There comes a point when we sit at the doorway to an opening in the path because we can't figure out how to get both ourselves and our burdens through. We may grow angry, bitter, or depressed as we see others passing through easily. But still we hold tightly to our burdens and will not fit through the opening. If our season of discouragement stems from this type of attitude, it is sad indeed. Sooner or later, we've got to let go. Why not make it sooner?

One Way Out

I like to picture the way out in the form of a cross. We know that the way is narrow, that to follow the Lord means taking up our cross and going after him. So the only way to leave the maze is by conforming ourselves to the cross the Lord has given us. That involves dropping every remaining burden, even the "noble" ones. Instead of lugging these about we must entrust them and ourselves to the God of love. Only then will we be truly free to follow the Lord. We will feel light and unencumbered when we reject the advice of the world to "do our own thing," and choose, instead, to follow the commission of Jesus: "Come. Follow me."

Jesus says that his yoke is easy and his burden light. A yoke has two sides to it. So if I am wearing a yoke that the Lord has placed on me, I can be certain that he is on the other side. If I'm wise, I'll walk at his pace, in the direction he leads. When the Lord gives me a burden, it may be quite different than one of my own choosing. When I carry a burden *I've* chosen, I must grasp it firmly, to be sure to keep hold of it. In the process I can't do much for anyone because all my energy is already directed to one end. Neither can I reach out a hand to receive help because my hands are full. But when the Lord gives me a burden, it's as if he fits a backpack snugly to my shoulders. I feel the weight of it and am often reminded of its presence and my need of rest and refreshment. But my hands are also free for other work and also free to reach out for help.

As we learn to lay down our own burdens to pick up those that the Lord gives us, we will experience victories that will affect our lives profoundly. They'll be at work deep within our spirits to form us according to his ways. Our ability to seek Jesus as our prize, our joy, and our gift will be greatly enhanced.

Early in our walk through the maze of faith, we may become so used to receiving exciting gifts that we keep looking forward to all the gifts we may receive along the way. And God will give us gifts to help us through the maze. But like a young child without patience to save up for the bike he really wants but settles instead for cheap gifts providing instant gratification, we may begin to seek the gifts rather than the giver. But as we work our way through the maze that God has designed for us, we will have every opportunity to grow in grace. Ours will be a pure-hearted search for the Shepherd who leads us and loves us so. We will be freer to love him in return, with a clear, unbounded, and generous heart, which is being transformed into a reflection of God's own heart.

Carrying Your Burdens the Right Way

If this sounds too otherworldly, let me clarify with some examples. Suppose a woman who has had three or four children becomes pregnant again. Suddenly the demands of her family seem too great to handle. The thought of another pregnancy has filled her with discouragement. She knows that her pregnancies tire her greatly. She thought that the Lord would not require this of her at this time. She begins to move through her days more slowly, discouraged by the thought of what lies ahead. Now, it is true that this woman is carrying a burden that is from the Lord and meant for her; but instead of carrying it in a backpack (or more correctly, in this case, a "frontpack"), she has picked up the burden with both hands. Holding it in her hands keeps it before her eyes always and prevents her from doing her daily work.

But what do you do if you just don't know how to put the burden at the Lord's altar, to let him adjust it in your pack in the proper way?

First, set aside a chunk of time to go before the Lord in prayer. Then read in Philippians about Jesus' perfect example of love. Though he was God, he did not hold on to the form of God, but "of his own free will he gave up all he had, and took the nature of a servant" (Phil 2:7). He became perfectly available to the Father. If Jesus, who is Lord of all the universe, can do this, surely we can do no less for our loving Creator than to be available for the work to which he has called us.

Remember to repent for trying to take control of your life. Ask God to give you an abiding trust in him. Be honest with the Lord about your feelings, expect struggle as part of your Christian life, and picture yourself giving your burden to the Lord. It may take awhile to work through this; you may need to go before the Lord repeatedly. But don't grow discouraged. Only remain faithful by asking and trusting the Lord for help. The Holy Spirit will work the truth that is in your head down into your heart, and remember, these are only eighteen inches apart.

Act on the Truth

Suppose a woman has had a lot of sickness in her family. Weeks go by, and she is unable to maintain her normal routine of household responsibilities, meetings, and recreation. Her discouragement mounts. Every time she starts to cheer up, some member of her family becomes sick again. The days drag on, and it becomes a great effort for her to pray, to act joyful or even civil. When she feels least like praying, she needs it the most. It is important that she base her behavior on the truth of scripture, rather than on how she's feeling at the moment. She should continue to pray daily. Taking her eyes off of the future, which seems to grow dimmer with each glance, she should ask the Lord for the strength and grace to live each day for his glory. She should continue to ask for healing for herself and her family; but if she must continue in this season a while longer, she should expect each day's grace to be sufficient, since no one can carry tomorrow's cross with today's grace. In short, she should realize that she is being tested. If she can learn the discipline of walking in faith when the going is difficult, when her feelings tell her to give up, she can experience significant growth. Romans says, "Let your hope keep you joyful, be patient in your troubles, and pray at all times" (12:12). Memorizing a passage such as this can enable her to shift her eyes from her burden so that the Lord can place it on her back.

It's Not Your Burden

Suppose that your sister divorces her husband. Because you love her, the divorce is always on your mind, eating away at your peace and raising barriers of discouragement in your relationship with the Lord. The burden of your sister's marriage hangs like a great weight around your neck.

In this instance, it is important to lay the burden at the Lord's altar and keep it there. You can't carry her burden. Clearly you need to support your sister, pray for her, and help her in ways appropriate to the situation. But the burden for the marriage is not yours. You should continue to go before the Lord if you find yourself picking up the burden again. The reactions of other family members are not your responsibility, either, even though you should pray for them and help them during this difficult time. Remember that you need support as well. It's difficult to watch one you love suffer, and if children are involved, the suffering is even greater.

Of course, if you're the one getting the divorce, you will need good counsel and support from a strong, reliable, and mature Christian to help you through this most difficult time. In a trial as severe as this, your burden will probably be constantly on your mind. Some situations in life, like divorce or the death of a loved one, run much deeper than the times of discouragement I am talking about in this chapter.

Nourished by the Word of God

The word of the Lord, which is truth, brings life to us. It is always a major source of encouragement in difficult times. When we are discouraged, we feel weak, thirsty, and empty. In our weakness the enemy will try to fill our thoughts with his lies. Instead, let us be fed by the word of God. One way to combat the lies of the enemy is to memorize meaningful scripture verses. We must be sure to take time for prayer and extra Bible reading during these times. One of my favorite encouragements comes from Isaiah. The passage begins with an address to Israel. I have substituted the word "sisters" for "Israel."

> Sisters, why then do you complain that the Lord doesn't know your troubles or care if you suffer injustice? Don't you know? Haven't you heard? The Lord is the everlasting God; he created all the world. He never grows tired or weary. No one understands his thoughts. He strengthens those who are weak and tired. Even those who are young grow weak; young men can fall exhausted. But those who trust in the Lord for help will find their strength renewed. They will rise on wings like eagles; they will run and not get weary; they will walk and not grow weak (Is 40:27-31).

Of course we are weak and must struggle against frustration and discouragement. That's part of the human predicament. But our secret as Christians (one that we can proclaim from the housetops) is that we are not expected to solve our problems on our own. God has not abandoned us, leaving us orphans. We have a Father of unimaginable love, who watches over us always. We have a mighty Lord who is also our brother. And we have within us the very Spirit of God, counseling, teaching, and refreshing us with the breath of life. If we let our thoughts dwell on these truths for awhile, they will pull us out of our discouragement. Our situation may look hopeless, but so did Jesus'. And never has a more hopeless situation been turned to greater victory. We are on his side, his sisters, who can expect that by his grace our trials will have as glorious an outcome. In retrospect, then, there's no greater day for hope than Holy Saturday.

How does discouragement relate to our prism lamps? A season of discouragement occurs when a cloud blocks the sun or when we forget to open the curtains to let the sun in. We become discouraged because the circumstances of our life, the room we are in, have become dark and drab; we no longer seem to reflect the beautiful colors that we once did. We forget that we are connected to a source of power that never fails. We need to remember to turn on the switch, to tap into the power that will restore us. As with all power sources, this one, too, has a price. It will cost us our life. But once again, the return is new life, and unlike the non-renewable sources most people depend on, this one will last forever.

SEVEN

Fear: A Crippling Way of Life

I have seen many women so afraid of losing or damaging their prisms that they wrap their lamps up to protect them. As a result, their prisms never reflect the light. If their lamps lie covered long enough, only dust will filter in. Perhaps an occasional storm will blow through an open window and saturate the lamp's coverings, causing mold and mildew. Only by throwing off the coverings and exposing the lamp to the light is there hope for restoration.

What can be done to bring the lamps into the light, to alleviate the suffering of women who feel trapped and encumbered by their fears? Of course everyone experiences fear occasionally, perhaps when a loved one is hospitalized with a serious illness. But I am talking about the kind of fear that is a way of life, a way of reacting to almost any outside stimuli. This kind of fear is a crippling condition, not a temporary experience.

Jesus does have a plan for removing the fear. His love and compassion, strength and courage can help us to take off the old coverings. There is hope for us all, whether we are only partially covered by fear or totally dominated by it. Whatever we have done to isolate or protect ourselves can be overcome by the powerful love of the risen Lord, the mercy of God our Father, and the wisdom of the Holy Spirit.

Facing Fear

With the knowledge that there is hope, let us go on to discuss how to recognize whether fear is entrapping you. Often, the problem is obscured by the fact that the fearful peson is operating with many layers of self-protective devices, which can blind them to their difficulty. However, certain telltale signs will indicate whether fear is crippling your life.

Do minor ailments disturb you so much that you become afraid of an undiagnosed rare disease, an unsuspected hidden condition, or death itself? Do you hope for a doctor's confirmation that will vindicate your concern and convince those around you that you really have been suffering? Do you experience almost chronic fatigue, which can sometimes make even the simplest tasks unbearable? Upon hearing of accidents that involve acquaintances, do you respond inwardly as though you were somehow responsible? Do you feel extremely uncomfortable in group situations, doing your best to avoid them or excuse yourself at the earliest opportunity, sometimes actually experiencing physical symptoms of sickness to explain your early departure? Are you fearful of losing your mind because you are constantly forgetting small things? Do minor irritations that others seem to take in stride become huge concerns to you, and do you find yourself attempting to justify your exaggerated reaction? Do you complain often, either in your mind or with your mouth? Has boredom become a way of life? In whatever you attempt, is perfection your goal? If you view a situation as overwhelming, are you careful not to begin the task lest you fail and suffer another blow to your self-esteem?

If you recognize yourself in many of these descriptions, you may also find yourself behaving in certain ways: you may be excessively dependent on others, seeking their advice or approval on even trivial matters, distrusting your own ability to make good decisions. You may get angry with yourself for acting this way. Perhaps you are always defensive, reacting with a sharp word or rudeness. You may even take the offensive, lest other people discover your weakness. Your attitude may be one of hopelessness or cynicism, if not publically then privately. And you may be prone to emotional outbursts.

This description may not apply to you, but fear does cripple people emotionally in just these ways. It can be devastating, perplexing, and confusing, both to the fearful person and to those she is near. But even if every situation I mentioned describes you in spades, Jesus can make you a strong, holy, and courageous woman. His love and his power are not limited by your weakness.

Handling Physical Symptoms

If you display physical symptoms of fear, be sure to consult a doctor. But before you do, pray that God will help you to trust your doctor. Ask the Lord to give him great wisdom and insight into your condition, even beyond his normal capabilities. If any laboratory tests are to be administered, pray that they will accurately reflect what is going on in your body. If necessary, seek a second opinion. At the same time, examine your life-style. Are you eating decent food and resting or sleeping a reasonable amount of time? Sleep may be difficult, which is why I also mentioned rest. If something shows up that can be treated medically, praise God and get treatment. But if your sleeping and eating patterns are sound and the doctor can find no organic basis for your complaints, you need to start believing that you're healthy. If the doctor says you're healthy, but you feel too tired to get dressed in the morning, tell your muscles to get moving anyway. If the dishes seem an insurmountable task, don't listen to the voice that says you can't do it. Tell your body it can surely stay up and moving for fifteen more minutes. Do all you can in that space of time, and then set yourself another goal. Think about how much you can accomplish, rather than how little. Instead of concentrating on your weakness, concentrate on the Lord's strength. Learning to believe your doctor can be an important step. It will probably take great effort on your part to do so, but the more you act on that belief, shaky though it may be, the more confidence you will have both in him, in yourself, and ultimately in God, for he is the one helping you to trust.

Three Sources of Fear

It helps to know certain spiritual principles that operate in this area so that you can hold on to, claim, and act upon them. Fear derives from the usual three sources, sometimes acting in concert with each other: the world, the flesh, and the devil. Recognizing these sources can help you to fight. Your experiences in life may have left you both scarred and scared. And the flesh in all of us is weak and sinful. Pride is often involved in the preoccupation with self that fear imposes on us. Also, our enemy, the devil, has either instigated this whole process or is doing all in his power to continue it in an effort to destroy us and everyone the Lord loves.

The enemy can be fought directly: "Resist the devil and he will flee" (Jas 4:7). A good way to fight is to picture your worst imaginable fear. Imagine Jesus in the middle of it, your strength and defender in battle no matter the danger—Jesus, from whom no power can ever separate us. He is our comfort, our rock, and our refuge. He will never leave us. Watching Jesus guide us through our worst fear will help us overcome the idea that we are helpless. I have often known women plagued by fears for whom this simple solution has brought great relief.

When our fears seem to be brought on by the world and difficult situations, past or present, it is helpful to meditate on scripture passages that show the Lord leading us victoriously through seemingly hopeless situations. The psalms are excellent sources for this, as are some of the major prophets. Consider Gideon. He was an unlikely hero. Yet God strengthened him and delivered Israel through him. Reflect on God's word and act on it. Memorize it. Let it become part of you. Listen to God's word rather than to your fears. If some scars haven't healed yet, have someone pray with you if possible. Remember that Jesus came to heal and restore. Pray daily for the gift of hope.

The last source of our fears stems from the flesh: from our own weakness and sin. It requires more explanation than the other two sources.

Fears can affect every facet of life. There are three distinct thrusts to these crippling fears and recognition of these can lead to a remedy for them. First, fear will almost always cover both sides of an issue. By this I mean that you may fear losing your job, but you also fear full employment. You may fear grave illness, but you also fear complete physical health. You may fear being with others, but you also fear being alone. You may fear an inactive, unfulfilling life, but also fear an active, involved life with all its attendant demands. An endless list of fears may bind you top and bottom, providing no escape. Even as I write this, I know that some who desperately want to escape from fear will fear the implications of that for their lives.

Second, people who are wrapped in fear may view themselves as inadequate and pitiful people almost beyond hope. But at the same time they may view themselves as quite superior to others. They may be painfully aware of their own shortcomings and also highly critical of others. Such a conflict within the person is bound to cause a great deal of turmoil.

Third, crippling fear either leads to a preoccupation with self or stems from a preoccupation with self. That, in a word, is pride.

This may sound bleak at first hearing. And without Jesus it is. But the good news is that Jesus came in power to set us free. He can change our minds, our hearts, our behavior, our lives.

Whether you recognize yourself in all the descriptions of fear or only one or two, the remedy is the same. If you feel bound by fear that seems to choke off full life with Jesus and your brothers and sisters, you can go back through the three aspects of fear and attack each one.

Overcoming Conflicting Fears

To fight the fact that fears will attack from both sides of an issue, three things are necessary. First, be forewarned so that you will be forearmed. If you fear losing your job, prayerfully consider whether you also fear keeping it. If so, look at the resulting conflict in your life. If it's affecting your behavior or thought life adversely, take steps to change that behavior.

Second, "let every thought become captive to the Lord, Jesus Christ" (2 Cor 10:5). Take that scripture seriously and, if necessary, repent for desiring to hold on to your own opinions about fears. Any fear except fear of the Lord or the kind of healthy fear that operates in a dangerous situation is a work of darkness and is to be done away with. Resist the desire to hang on to any particular fear and begin to hand your fears over to the Lord. Pray for strength and courage. Ask God to help you discipline your mind, so that when fearful thoughts begin to overshadow you, you can rebuke them, tell them to leave in the name of Jesus, and fill your mind with a psalm, a favorite scripture, a song, or the task at hand.

Third, begin to act on the truth, not on your fears. As Paul says, "Do not be conformed to this world but be transformed by the renewal of your mind, that you may prove what is the will of God, what is good and acceptable and perfect (Rom 12:2). By acting out a life of pleasing service, our minds will be transformed. Don't wait until your mind is transformed to begin to act on God's ways. Act first to whatever extent you can, and, like a rusty piece of machinery needing oil, you will begin to be renewed. Tell your muscles to move and make them obey. If cleaning the bathroom seems an overwhelming task, rely on the truth that, even if you are not able, you can do it in the strength of Jesus. Force yourself to work twenty minutes for the glory of God. View even mundane tasks like getting dressed or getting up as service for God's glory. When you are tempted to react angrily over a trivial matter, especially when it does not involve wrongdoing, then keep quiet for God's honor and glory. Be on guard in these situations, that you do not lapse into self-righteousness. Do not excuse or overlook unrighteous behavior, simply dismissing it by saying that you are now above being bothered by it. Be quick to forgive and be reconciled if that is needed, or to forebear in patience out of love for him who forbears with you. For it is possible to exhibit the right behavior for the wrong motives. In all things we must strive to do what we do for the honor and glory of the Father.

By doing these three things—being forewarned and forearmed about the dual nature of your fears, taking your thoughts captive to Jesus, and acting on the basis of the truth rather than on your fears, you can go a long way toward being rid of the fear that can cripple you. But please be patient with yourself. You did not acquire the problem overnight and it will take a while to be rid of it. Work on developing a sense of humor about yourself. If you fail in something, try again. Your aim should be to replace old habits of fear with new ones of trust. It will be difficult, of course. You may not like your old habits, but at least you're used to them. New habits require stepping on to unfamiliar territory. You don't know what to expect. But take courage! You will not step out alone. There is one who stands before you and beside you, who will carry you over the roughest spots. The Father wants to set you free so you can follow his son and be full of confidence. He will supply every grace you need to begin, to endure, and to be victorious.

Pray for Humility

The way to fight the tendency to view yourself as either a complete wretch or vastly superior to others is twofold. First, pray for a gift of true humility, that you may see yourself as you are: a person with some strengths and some weaknesses who stands in need of a savior. When you are tempted to wail about how wretched and horrible you are, remember the truth in Hosea, chapter 7: "They have not prayed to me sincerely, but instead they throw themselves down and wail as the heathen do" (7:14)

Hosea is describing people who cry out hopelessly, without realizing who they cry to. It is a necessary, right, and humble act to cry out to the Lord. But to behave as though we alone among all of creation are beyond hope is an act of pride. Our cry as Christians should be one of pain, but also of confidence. For although we stand before the Father as sinners, we know that we have been purchased at a great price. Therefore, we dare to call God, "Father." Let us know and act on the knowledge that although we are not able, God is; although we are weak and helpless, he is strong and victorious and will share the victory with us. We truly have an enabling God.

Second, practice the kind of self-forgetfulness that leads to love and service for others. Break the habit of making comparisons, which leaves you either discouraged or self-righteous. Read Romans, chapter 12, until the words give flesh and meaning to your own life. When you find yourself making comparisons or thinking critically of others, be quick to repent and to receive forgiveness. Ask the Spirit to point out to you the times when you begin to act or think wrongly so that you can more quickly form the good habits of self-forgetfulness and charitable thought.

Self-Forgetfulness: The Remedy for Pride

To deal with fear that either stems from or leads to a preoccupation with self, you should first repent of pride. Remember that repentance is a joyful grace. Rather than something to run away from, it is the easiest way to full life. Repentance always hurts my pride. But I'm glad when the solution is so simple.

If you suffer from preoccupation with self, you may have to repent of pride that would make you resist wanting to change; pride that thinks Jesus is not powerful enough to overcome problems as deeply rooted as yours. Pride often tempts you to look for easier answers than a renewal of your mind and heart. It leads you into self-preoccupation so that you view yourself as either extraordinarily abject or as superior to others. Thank God for the grace of repentance, and be quick to accept his healing forgiveness.

If you cannot initially bring yourself to pray for forgiveness, then pray for the grace to repent. At whatever place you find yourself, begin to move in the direction that leads to life—to Jesus who is the Way, the Truth, and the Life. If we call ourselves Christians, if we believe in him who has come to set us free, let us begin now to follow the path he has set before us.

Consider this passage from Mark's gospel:

> Then Jesus called the crowd and his disciples to him. "If anyone wants to come with me," he told them, "he must

forget himself, carry his cross, and follow me. For whoever wants to save his own life will lose it; but whoever loses his life for me and for the gospel will save it. Does a person gain anything if he wins the whole world but loses his life? Of course not! There is nothing he can give to regain his life. If a person is ashamed of me and of my teaching in this godless and wicked day, then the Son of Man will be ashamed of him when he comes in the glory of his Father with the holy angels" (8:34-38).

We must repent of our preoccupation with self and desire true self-forgetfulness. In today's world Jesus' words sound perhaps even more antagonistic than they did when he first spoke them. But they are just as true, despite contemporary, psychological theories that tell us the opposite. Lest we doubt that Jesus himself is the key to our freedom, he offers the strong admonition of the last verse in this passage.

Once you have begun the work of repentance, what must you do to replace the time, effort, and thought put into your old way of behaving? Consider the following passage from Matthew: "While Jesus was eating, a woman came to him with an alabaster jar filled with an expensive perfume, which she poured on his head. This disciples saw this and became angry. 'Why all this waste?' they asked. 'This perfume could have been sold for a large amount and the money given to the poor'" (26:7-9).

This woman was extravagant in her love and generosity. Her act of pouring out the expensive perfume expressed her self-forgetfulness in the face of her love for another and symbolized a heart poured out for love of Jesus. It must have taken considerable love and courage to walk into Simon's house to perform her service of love. Her extravagance upset even the disciples. But Jesus rebuked them, saying that wherever the gospel was preached, her kindness would be retold.

What a great example for us. It is only in forgetting about ourselves and our desire to save ourselves that we can be saved. Our world today isn't much different from this woman's. Sin still abounds. If you want to save your life, you're told to look out for "number one," which means you must protect yourself from others who might try to encroach upon your freedom to express yourself, to do your own thing, to fulfill yourself. But the words of Jesus come ringing down the centuries as true, though just as inimical to the voice of the world: "For whoever wants to save his own life will lose it; but whoever loses his life for my sake will save it" (Mt 16:25).

Look to Jesus. Ask him how you can pour out your life for his sake. You may have to begin small; after all, you may have to learn a whole new way of life. You will experience setbacks; but don't put off the journey for fear. Dare to try and dare to fail, to repent and to begin again. It is part of our condition that we are weak, and it is to God's glory that we repent and pick ourselves up, accepting forgiveness and moving on. Those prisms hanging covered and protected will someday sparkle brilliantly in the sun, reflecting the glory of their creator and restorer. Begin now by giving thanks to the God who made you, the God who is victorious and who will deliver you. Pray for a grateful heart in all circumstances, trusting not in your own ability to overcome but in him who has already overcome.

Part II

Making Love Real

God wants every woman to become whole, holy, and strong. That's part of his plan. To cooperate with it, we should take a look at our attitudes, feelings, and responses, knowing that the Holy Spirit can make up for the deficiencies in us. Yet to stop here would be to fall short of real fulfillment. We have yet to taste the richest joy that comes from belonging wholly to God.

Just as Christ poured out his love for us in countless acts both great and small, so we should pour out his love to others. Our aim is not to feel loved or loving but to act in a loving way. Women are uniquely blessed with the opportunity to act out love in many practical ways, often through all the details involved in caring for their husbands and children. The world sees this responsibility as a drudgerous burden. But in reality it is a cause for great rejoicing. We have a share in the divine plan, a plan that makes no sense to a wicked world—die to self and you will find life. And it would seem folly to us, too, if Jesus had not paved the way, pouring out his own life and declaring: "A new commandment do I give you; that you love one another as I have loved you" (Jn 13:34).

It's time to shift our attention away from ourselves so that we can consider how to live out this commandment. For as we forget ourselves in order to think of others, God's kingdom will come among us. Our every action will reflect the good news of his saving love.

EIGHT

Service Love

"The road to hell is paved with good intentions!" How many times have we heard that expression? I heard it often as I was growing up. Like most human beings, my spirit was willing but my flesh was weak. I would come up with a great idea about doing something nice for someone, relishing the thought of the good deed and the delightful effect it would have on others. But that was usually as far as it went. My great ideas seldom got translated into reality.

When my mother began to work outside the home, I knew it wasn't easy for her to care for the family and work at the same time. I thought it would be wonderful if she could return to a thoroughly scrubbed house, freshly waxed floors, and a hot supper cooking on the stove. That may even have happened once or twice. Usually, however, I would procrastinate until it was all I could do to perform my regular chores before my mother got home.

Of course Mom understood what was going on. After hearing about my great plans and the accompanying apology (I wanted her to know my heart was in the right place), she would sigh and say, "Yes, Ruth, that would have been nice. I'm glad you were thinking of me. But be careful and remember, the road to hell is paved with good intentions."

That hurt, but it was effective. Scripture makes the point that love is much more than good intentions when it says, "Our love should not just be words and talk; it must be true love, which shows itself in action" (1 Jn 3:18).

Unfortunately, Mom's warning had little impact on me. Though I felt kindly and lovingly disposed, I seemed unable to translate my feelings into action. When Mom was home, I was even worse. I liked to plan the extra work as a surprise, but if I couldn't carry it out without any element of constraint, it didn't sound like fun at all. I'm afraid that I was not often a cheerful worker.

By the time I reached college, I had become disciplined in my studies to some extent. I enjoyed most of my courses and always had my assignments ready on time. But life in a dorm did nothing to help me form good practical habits for my life. My room often looked like a disaster area. When I met Russ, I was very impressed with his ability to make decisions and follow through on them. He was a hard worker, fulfilling his course requirements and working as a night watchman besides. Yet he found time for recreation as well. I was probably all the more attracted to him because I sensed that I lacked these qualities.

After becoming engaged to Russ, I was determined to learn to think in more practical terms. How else would I be able to get along with such a practically minded husband? Actions were still not uppermost in my mind, but my decision to change was a sign of progress. I began to pray every day for a practical mind.

I spent the summer after my engagement with a small group of dedicated Christians who were involved in "street evangelism." It was a time when I experienced the tremendous faith and love of a body of Christians. While I was with them I learned something very key to my growth as a Christian. Fran, one of the most open, wise, and loving people I had ever met, would always say, "Let's go beyond meeting needs. Let's work and pray to anticipate them."

This impressed me deeply. I could see that Fran actually lived in a way that touched the hearts of those around her, including myself. At the same time, I knew that I only met others' needs in the most casual and offhand way. I'd never thought much about meeting others' needs. I'd been too preoccupied with my own. Even the times when I actually surprised my mother were motivated to a great extent by the reward I would experience as a result of pleasing my mother.

So I began to pray for a practical mind. Whenever I failed, I would repent and decide to pray harder. Gradually I began to improve. On my good days I would remember to tell my eyes to be watchful and my body to be quick to respond to the needs of others. Finally I began to experience the connection between good intentions and practical thoughts and actions.

At the end of the summer, however, I returned to college and was once again caught up in a world of books and study. By spring, I was making wedding plans. The importance of having a practical mind had faded considerably. I was young and in love, blithely confident that our love would see us through every difficulty and immensely ignorant of the fact that any of the difficulties might include adjusting to each other—the practical, hard-working realist and the impractical but dedicated idealist.

We were married while both of us were still in school and working. It soon became evident that I needed more than a kindly, warm and loving feeling to get me through the day. I needed a practical and organized mind, a hard-working body, and enough love to count it all joy. It was a crucible of work, frustration, and joy for at least five years. I was learning new ways to be and to live, but I was often confused and unhappy. Then I had the opportunity to attend a course taught in the Christian community of which I am a member. It's called servant school, and it consists of teachings from the Bible on service love, combined with plenty of opportunities to apply what we learned. As a study guide we used *The Normal Christian Worker*, by Watchman Nee.

After I took the course and performed the tasks assigned to me, I began to shed my old attitudes toward work, ones that had made me so confused and unhappy. Fran's words and my mother's words came back to me, and I could see that I needed to take on a whole new ideal of loving. Since then I've come to understand that many of my old attitudes about love and service are shared by nearly everyone. That's why I want to let others know what I have learned so that they may grow as well.

Serving as Women

All Christians are called to serve, to lay down their lives for one another. How we are called to serve will depend on our state in life and the Lord's specific plan for our lives. But as women, especially those called to be wives and mothers, our service is clear. We are often engaged in very personal, direct service. We meet others' most basic needs—for food preparation, cleanliness, care of clothes, and shelter—all the while smoothing hurts and difficulties and offering emotional support to others. Some of us must also earn the money to provide food, shelter, and clothing for our families. We must be able to see needs, respond to them, and anticipate them. If we don't, chaos will ensue.

We can see the baby's need for clean diapers, but we can respond to it only if we've anticipated his need by having the diapers laundered before the last one is used up. We can respond to our family's need for food by preparing a meal by the time they're hungry. And of course we've had to shop for the food in the first place.

Jesus' Example

We know that Jesus came to serve, but his way of serving (at least before his Passion) might seem glamorous to us by comparison with the repetitive, mundane chores we perform. Yet, he raised the status of personal service forever. Every time he allowed himself to be diapered and fed as a baby, every time his face got scrubbed and his ears got cleaned, every time his nose got wiped and his clothes got washed he sanctified our service as mothers. And, as a final sign to us forever, he did the job of the most menial slave on the night before he died. He washed the dirty feet of the apostles, who had been tramping around the dusty streets of Jerusalem all day. Jesus spent his life denying himself, taking up his cross, and following his

Father. It is our joy and privilege as women to be given the opportunity to do the same, both in the small and great services and sacrifices of our lives.

If that sounds nice but hardly the way you view your work, you have loads of company. Seven years ago I couldn't have said these things. I didn't think it was practical to live your life that way, but God is faithful in purifying his people. He has shown me that my inability to take joy in the midst of my daily routine wasn't the fault of the work or of the members of my family. It was rooted in wrong attitudes within myself. Once I began to repent of my old attitudes toward service and learned to live according to a new set of principles, I began to experience a new freedom and enjoyment in the midst of my days. My chores were no longer hateful tasks that I had to accomplish before going on to more fulfilling pursuits. Instead they became my work, the willing offering of my hands and heart to God. I learned to clean my house with the attitude that I was cleaning the courts of the King. I prepared food as if I were going to serve it to those who have gone before us in faith and were at the banquet of the Lord. I laundered clothes and ran errands as if for the Holy Family. I knew that it was a privilege to be called to serve in the kingdom of God. At first I had to force myself to think this way. But before long I discovered that the Lord had indeed changed my mind and heart. I still struggle sometimes, but I know what to guard against. I simply refuse to give up the joy I experience from serving with the right heart. What are some attitudes toward service to guard against?

Serving Myself

If I serve only in ways that I enjoy, without considering the needs of those around me, I'm missing the mark. It's fine, even desirable, to enjoy what I'm doing. But if that's the only reason I do it, then I'm probably consistently neglecting other services or doing them only grudgingly. If so, I am actually serving myself, not anyone else.

For instance, what if I attend a potluck with my family and

volunteer to serve in the kitchen because I enjoy talking with the other women? Meanwhile my toddler is wreaking havoc in the other room by walking around the tables and pulling all the silverware off them. In this case, my service is actually hindering the work of others. I need to fulfill my own responsibilities first before tackling additional ones. Until my child is a bit older, the most effective and loving way for me to serve is to keep an eye on him.

Or suppose that I really enjoy making pies but that my family prefers cookies. If I continue to make pies despite this, I'm only serving myself. I may even resent my family for not appreciating my efforts enough.

Serving to Receive Approval

Our aim should not be to serve others so that they will love us. That puts the focus on us again. Of course it's great to be appreciated and encouraged in our work. But when it comes to housework it's always easier to notice what hasn't been done rather than what has. If I've served all day hoping for a "pat on the head," I'm likely to be disappointed. Consider this parable:

> Suppose one of you has a servant who is plowing or looking after the sheep. When he comes in from the field, do you tell him to hurry along and eat his meal? Of course not! Instead, you say to him, "Get my supper ready, then put on your apron and wait on me while I eat and drink; after that you may have your meal." The servant does not deserve thanks for obeying orders, does he? It is the same with you; when you have done all you have been told to do, say, "We are ordinary servants; we have only done our duty"
> (Lk 17:7-10).

It's true. We don't deserve thanks. We are not looking for approval but for a righteous life. However, when Jesus told this parable, I don't believe that he meant to say that we should be stingy in giving approval and encouragement to others. He was talking about the correct attitude for a servant to have. Jesus loves a home where support, affirmation, and encouragement are generously given to all. But the point is that we should not be seeking it. We shouldn't let the desire for approval motivate our work.

Competition

Competitive serving is another barrier to serving with love and joy. Often it is an outgrowth of serving for approval. I may want to be known as a hard worker, but may fear the laziness within me. So I serve industriously to overcome it. I may take pride in the fact that I can stay at a job longer and do it more thoroughly than anyone else. My house must be neater, my kitchen counters brighter, my floors shinier than my friends' or neighbors'. I may act modest about my accomplishments but still be very competitive inside. Just let someone start to interfere with my daily work, with the pattern I've set up, and I will quickly learn whether I have served because I want life to be more pleasant for my family or because I want the cleanest house on the block.

Industriousness shouldn't be confused with competitiveness. We should strive to do the best job we can because we are servants of a great King. We want to do a good job for him. If we compare our homes to others, we may feel devastated if ours doesn't seem as orderly. Such an approach fails to take into account the fact that the circumstances and priorities of each woman's life will be different from every other woman. Whenever I find myself thinking that perhaps I should do something more like another woman does it, I stop and weigh the decision against two criteria: Will it establish more order? Will it help me attain the goal of peace within my home?

If our desire for perfection makes people feel on edge when they are home, we're probably demanding too much. On the other hand, if there's such disorder that no one ever knows where to find anything, we're probably not doing enough to maintain order. Of course, just because the family finds our requirements difficult doesn't mean we're being too stringent. Depending on the children's ages and our husband's willingness to participate, it may help if the family talks together at some point about how best to attain the goals of peace and order in the home.

Getting Organized

Procrastination and disorganization are enemies of true service. When I was newly married, I used to go to the grocery store after first checking the specials in the paper and making my list accordingly. However, I was continually running back to the store during the week to buy items that I hadn't noticed I needed. For instance, I would begin to fix stew only to find that I was out of onions. To remedy this situation I started making a weekly menu, checking my cookbooks to make sure I had the necessary spices and ingredients. I wasn't experienced enough as a cook to make dinner from whatever I happened to have on hand. Once I had everything, I could even make meals ahead of time. A simple meal schedule saved time and money and freed me from feeling pressured when I was cooking meals.

I've also found that it helps to know ahead of time which days will work best to do washing or cleaning. Scheduling can be a useful tool for peaceful service.

The Only Right Motive Is Love

Service love consists not just of words, but of actions. It is important that we not simply feel kind, but we must act out of kindness. We kid ourselves if we think that we love our brother or sister in Cambodia, if we cannot act kindly toward a brother or sister, husband or child, whom we see everyday. Serving with the right heart is crucial. Our attitudes and motives are very important if we want to live in the kingdom of God. St. Paul reminds us, "I may give away everything I have, and even give up my body to be burned—but if I have no love, this does me no good" (1 Cor 13:3). It's incredible to think that anything but love would prompt me to give up my life. And yet I might be motivated by bitterness, revenge, or pride to perform all the little tasks in which I "lay dowlife" every day. Each of us gives our life in hundreds of little ways every day. Does love motivate us or does something else? Do we try to manipulate others, under the theory that if we give up something, we will be in a better bargaining position later?

We must be very careful. We can give up our lives for many reasons, but if it's not done from love of God and the brethren, our sacrifice does us no good. Scripture is clear. It's words are sobering on this point. But let us be encouraged by remembering that our hope is Jesus. Let us keep our eyes on him who leads us in the paths of righteousness. He will strengthen and comfort us, filling our hearts with his love if we will but humbly ask his help.

Self-Pity

One of the greatest obstacles to true service is self-pity. It's the most destructive of all the blocks to faithful service of the Lord. First, it fixes our attention inward. We cannot see others' needs when all we can see is our own. Second, in order to put our eyes on ourselves, we've got to take them off Jesus, our only hope and reason to serve.

To be a wife and mother is hard work. Very often everyone around us will be depending on us to be strong. In the midst of this, it can be easy to lose sight of our calling to serve in the body of Christ. We may be tempted to feel sorry for ourselves.

The first letter of John reminds us about our responsibility to love God and our brothers. "For he cannot love God, whom he has not seen, if he does not love his brother, whom he has seen" (1 Jn 4:20). The kind of self-sacrificing, sacramental love that Jesus practiced would be impossible for us were it not for the Holy Spirit dwelling in us. "For our love for God means that we obey his commands. And his commands are not too hard for us, because every child of God is able to defeat the world. And we win the victory over the world by means of our faith. Who can defeat the world? Only the person who believes that Jesus is the Son of God" (1 Jn 5:3-5).

With God's strength and power, we can serve well and lovingly. But when we try to serve from our own strength things will go haywire. When we rely on our strength rather than on the Giver of Strength, then pride has crept in. At that point our motives or attitudes have already gotten off the track. After that, it becomes easier to fall prey to the other wrong motives or attitudes we've discussed. Whenever we take our eyes off Jesus, they will quickly focus on ourselves. By then we've become an easy target for self-pity.

> "Why does he get to watch the ball game while I have to do the dishes?"
>
> "He always gets to do the fun things with the kids, and I always end up with the nasty jobs. It isn't fair!"
>
> "Helen has a new kitchen and here I am stuck in a kitchen that looks worse than hers did before it was redone."
>
> "Everybody has time to do what they want except me."
>
> "Nobody really appreciates what I do around here."
>
> "Nobody ever really appreciates me just for myself."

There may be some truth in some of these thoughts, but letting them run through our minds unattended is like sending the Pied Piper to march through Hamlin. Like rats following the Piper, other bitter and self-pitying thoughts will begin to parade through our minds until we are convinced that we are one of the most abused women alive. Now, we know that this isn't the truth and that God doesn't want us to think this way. Remember the psalmist's wise words, "When my thoughts were bitter and my feelings were hurt, I was as stupid as an animal; I did not understand you" (Ps 73:21-22).

We might be verging on self-pity when someone in our family makes a joke or an innocent remark that ignites the poison within us. Infuriated that our family cannot even have the decency to see that we are suffering, we may start slamming doors, yelling, crying, making sarcastic remarks, or sulking—depending on how we choose to make our feelings known. This kind of scene seldom helps anyone. Besides getting at the real problem that triggered the attack of self-pity, our families, and especially our husbands, will first have to wade through all the garbage we've spewed out in our anger.

If we always respond to difficulties this way, working things through can be compounded by past experiences. We may be discouraged, thinking that we could never change. But we should never for a moment forget that our hope is in the Lord. He is strong, patient, wise, and merciful enough to help us change. But we won't change if we're constantly thinking about the way that everyone else ought to change. We will only make life more difficult for ourselves. Instead, let us place ourselves before the living God, whose ways are not ours, and whose thoughts are not ours. If we are to follow his example, we will spend our lives giving to others. Let us pray that we may be in the center of his will. We are not worthless creatures. We've been ransomed for the greatest price ever paid and have been made worthy by God himself. We don't serve grudgingly but because it's our privilege to imitate Jesus in all things. And we can do this through the power of the Holy Spirit, who enables us to do all things with joy.

Fighting Self-Pity

These are some of the ways you can combat self-pitying thoughts when you sense that you're falling into that trap.

Refuse to let such thoughts run through your mind. Choose strength and not weakness: "I want to be a strong and holy woman, Lord. Please keep these thoughts far from me, for they bring only death, but you bring life." It takes time and practice and grace to discipline your mind. But don't become discouraged. You *can* do it.

When you seem too tired to get through a task, you don't necessarily need to figure out why things seem so difficult right then. Overtiredness can destroy anyone's sense of perspective. Try instead to persevere, to think of other things until you have gotten some rest. The next day you may discover that something in your life or relationship does need to be straightened out, but chances are you won't even remember why you were so upset.

If a self-pitying thought runs through your head, confront it with God's truth. If laying down your life seems unfair at the moment, so be it. It was unfair when Jesus laid down his, too. Pray instead, "Lord, help me to have your heart of obedience and peace while I finish this work."

Sometimes it will be harder than others to quiet troublesome thoughts. Try to sing, or put on a Christian record to remind yourself that God's in control.

It can help to thank God for every part of the task at hand. "Thank you for this bread, Lord, and thank you that you have blessed us with such an enjoyable lunch. Thank you for my health, that I am strong enough to prepare this food. Thank you for the health of my husband and children, that they can eat this food and be strengthened by it. Thank you for football and the enjoyment it brings my husband. Help me to learn to appreciate it and to enjoy watching the rest of the game with him. Thank you for this day which you have made and blessed by your presence. Thank you for your lordship over my life." By this time the job is done. You feel good about it and good about yourself and your husband, and you can go on with your day with a much lighter heart. A thankful heart is always the most powerful weapon against self-pity.

Finally, you can remind yourself that Jesus has called you to be like him and you have committed yourself to following him. Remember that even Jesus had to fight temptations to self-pity. If anyone had a right to give in to them he did. But we know that he didn't sin. Can you picture him acting bitterly, sulking, pouting, making sarcastic comments, and slamming doors? The thought is enough to make us laugh. It reminds us of how weak and silly we can be and how much we need God's grace. Let us be restored to the Father by repenting of any pride, which makes us susceptible to temptation to begin with.

In Romans, Paul tells us to "take up the weapons of the Lord Jesus Christ, and stop paying attention to your sinful nature and satisfying its desires" (Rom 13:14). The tendency toward self-pity is part of our sinful nature. We even enjoy it to some extent. The best way to fight it is head on. We should be on the offensive against self-pitying thoughts. If we try to run from them, they will chase after us. But if we turn and fight with grateful hearts in the power of our brother, Jesus, they will flee, and we will be set free to serve God and give him glory with our minds and bodies. Always, we work for his glory. It is part of his plan that we serve well and gladly, even if only to bend over and tie a shoe with a smile on our faces.

Service love is like a light in our prism lamps. Our prisms may still be getting cleaned and polished to reflect God's glory, but when we are serving others with glad and grateful hearts, the light and love of God pours out of us and touches every prism of our personality, lighting up and making beautiful every aspect of our characters. People should "see" how we love one another, not just hear about it. With God's grace we can lay down our lives for one another, giving glory to the Father by doing so.

NINE

Food: A Source of Peace or Division?

Women show love to their families in countless practical ways. One way to love others is expressed through the food that we prepare for them. It is the most basic, regular, and time-consuming of the ways we serve. That's why I want to spend some time reflecting on our attitudes toward food preparation. Is food a positive force toward the development of peace and joy within our homes, or is it something that divides and aggravates the members?

I grew up hearing the old expression, "The way to a man's heart is through his stomach." That seemed like a funny route to me, and I never took the saying too seriously. But after I was married I realized that there was more wisdom in that saying than I had first supposed. I quickly discovered the value of providing the kind of good, solid meals my husband preferred. I had only been married a few weeks when my husband's aunt repeated that saying to me. I have learned many things about food and my family since then, but I haven't forgotten the essential truth that food choice and preparation is one of the most basic ways I can love my family. It's worth taking great care to be faithful in doing it.

Regarding food as a means for loving and serving others will mean that we will need to put aside our own preferences in this area. We may sometimes need to cook foods that we dislike preparing or eating. It may even mean at times that we forego preparing certain kinds of food, as when an expert piemaker decides to refrain from baking pies while her husband is on a diet. Our decisions regarding food will have to be weighed against the fundamental principle of service love.

Deciding about Food

It can be difficult to make good decisions about the best way to provide pleasing and nutritious meals for our families. We've grown up with certain ideas about food and with definite likes and dislikes. We read so much about the need to be careful of cancer-causing substances, preservatives, food colors, and processing that destroy food value. We know that heart problems can be caused by obesity and too much cholesterol. We're bombarded daily by advertising promoting prepackaged foods in ways that make them seem irresistable, socially acceptable, time- or energy-saving, and gullet-gratifying. In addition to all this, we may be trying to keep or get our body in shape for health and beauty's sake. And of course we're probably trying to save money as well. No wonder we think about food a lot! No wonder we talk about it at such length!

We can study nutrition, talk with other women about how they serve their families, and consider the things we like to prepare and eat. But our decisions can't be based just on these things. Our own family's needs should be uppermost in our minds. If we cook with a great deal of garlic and hot pepper, despite the fact that members of our family have trouble digesting food prepared this way, then we are not serving them as we should. To serve the family well, we've got to consider our budgets, our husbands' preferences, our children's preferences—and also our own. There's nothing wrong with occasionally cooking something that we especially like. We're a member of the family, too.

But what if everyone has different tastes? First we should consider our husband's tastes. If a wife can please her husband, she's on the right track. But what about everyone else's tastes? In an effort to solve this problem, one woman I know decided to fix bland food, putting spices on the table so every member of her large family could please themselves. Another option would be to fix meals each day of the week that reflect the tastes of particular members of the family. Or we might want to institute "experiment night," a night in which everyone can try a new dish with the aim of enlarging their likes and experiences.

We should also be sensitive to what really will serve our families. If someone is trying to lose weight and we bake cakes for them, we aren't really loving them. If we want to love them in a special way, we could do it better by participating in one of their favorite activities with the rest of the family. If that's not possible, we could find something else to do to show our love—mend clothes, iron a daughter's dress, or take our son's radio to the repair shop. Depending on age and taste, there are many ways to show love other than by preparing food.

One reason why we focus on food as an expression of love is that it has been associated with comfort and reward from our childhood. When babies cry we pick them up, change them, and feed them. Of course the child is greatly comforted. We all had that experience when we were infants. And as mothers we have had the reward of a happy baby.

As children grow, they become more vocal about what kind of food they like and dislike. As they try new foods they will often respond either with delight or with "I don't like that!" That puts us in a difficult spot. We want to please our families, but we realize that they often prefer things that aren't good for them. It is important for our own mental health to think carefully about the food we prepare and to stick with the choices we make. Otherwise, food will only cause tension and division.

Let's take stock of what we've discussed thus far. Our attitude needs to be positive. We are to nurture our family in love. In doing so, we will need to take our husband's preferences and our children's tastes into account as well as our budget and the laws of good nutrition. Time is also a factor, especially if we work outside the home. When we do, we often must simply accept the fact that we may not have the time or energy to fix the meals we would like to. Instead, we will need to learn how to cut corners.

Whenever we make decisions concerning food, we should consider the complex needs of our families. We should make sure than our plans meet with our husbands' approval. Our attitude should be to seek God's will for our lives. If we believe it is right to eat only "natural" foods but our husbands and families think otherwise, then we should drop our plan in order to serve them. To everything there is a season, and perhaps some day we will be able to cook more in accordance with our own tastes and beliefs, but for now we should put aside our own preferences.

Romans, chapter 14, can help us understand the attitudes we should have towards food. It reminds us of the importance of choosing food with our families' total needs in mind.

> Far from passing judgment on each other, therefore, you should make up your mind never to be the cause of your brother tripping or falling. Now I am perfectly aware, of course, and I speak for the Lord Jesus, that no food is unclean in itself; however, if someone thinks that a particular food is unclean, then it is unclean for him. And indeed if your attitude to food is upsetting your brother, then you are hardly being guided by charity. You are certainly not free to eat what you like if that means the downfall of someone for whom Christ died.
>
> In short, you must not compromise your privilege, because the kingdom of God does not mean eating or drinking this or that, it means righteousness and peace and joy brought by the Holy Spirit. If you serve Christ in this way you will please men and be respected by men. So let us adopt any custom that leads to peace and our mutual improvement (Rom 14:13-18).

Paul was addressing his remarks to a Christian community, which most of us do not live in. However, our families can be considered small communities, and we must be careful not to let food destroy the peace that God wants to establish among us. If our husbands want butter rather than margarine, we should buy it. If they want cream rather than milk, we should comply with their wishes. If they want meat and potatoes, rather than casseroles, then let's cook that way. The converse is also true. If we prefer steaks but our husbands want casseroles, we should learn to prepare them with love. Ideally, our husbands will learn to trust our management of this area so well that they will be free to delight in us as helpmates.

Speaking of Food

The way we speak about food can be important. We hear so much talk now about how much damage we can do by eating the wrong things. We can create too many fat cells in our babies if we over-feed them. We can aggravate allergies by using foods with chemical preservatives. If we don't eat organically grown food, pesticides will damage us. There seems to be no end to the possible pitfalls.

If we are taking these and other things into account and cooking in a way that is basically acceptable to our family, even though it may include some of the foods we've heard are potentially harmful, we need not feel guilty. As Paul says, "Happy is the person who does not feel guilty when he does something he judges right" (Rom 14:22).

But we can really make one another feel guilty by the way we discuss food. Remember what scripture says: "You then, who eat only vegetables—why do you pass judgment on your brother? And you who eat anything—why do you despise your brother? All of us will stand before God to be judged by him" (Rom 14:10). We should realize that other women have had to decide the best way to nurture their families, just as we have. We have no right to judge the way another woman feeds her family, except, perhaps, in a case of malnourishment, when through ignorance a woman fails to feed her family properly. However, most of us won't be faced with such a situation. We should take the scripture's advice: "Keep what you believe about this matter, then, between yourself and God" (Rom 14:22).

I was astonished the first time I read this verse and began to understand the implication for my own speech. Why shouldn't we talk about our opinions? Paul mentions some of the reasons in earlier verses: "So then, we must always aim at those things that bring peace and that help strengthen one another. Do not, because of food, destroy what God has done" (Rom 14:19-20).

We must be careful to make peace our aim when discussing food. Can we talk about food at all? Yes, certainly. It's helpful to share recipes and ideas, not however in a way that promotes ours as *the right way*. It's fine to discuss why we've made the choices we have, realizing that our reasons may not fit into another family's pattern of life. We should keep this passage from Romans in mind when tempted to judge another: "Who are you to judge the servant of someone else? It is his own Master who will decide whether he succeeds or fails. And he will succeed, because the Lord is able to make him succeed" (Rom 14:4).

If we take these words to heart, we will be careful not only of what we say, but how we say it. If a woman shares some decisions she has made for her family about food and we respond "Really?" our tone of voice could imply happy excitement, doubt, or even scorn. A raised eyebrow can devastate as quickly as a word of rebuff. Yet if our heart is right, our words, tone of voice, and facial expressions will also be right.

If we've examined ourselves in the area of speech and been found wanting, remember, we don't need to walk around with the "big G" on our chests. Let's just repent and ask for God's mercy and help. We might also ask forgiveness from people we may have offended. We should let God's Spirit lead us in these matters.

Food and Celebration

Times of celebration are important to our lives, and we can do a lot to further the unity of our family by carefully planning the foods we prepare for such days. If we've had the right attitudes toward food all along, our times of celebration will be all the more joyous. Thanksgiving dinner with all the trimmings inspires us to give more thanks to God if we have not been eating that way every day. A fancy birthday cake with ice cream is a real cause for rejoicing when cakes are not commonplace in our diet. We might let everyone have whatever they'd like for breakfast, lunch, and dinner on their birthdays. When something really works we might try it again the next year. Before you know it, we've created a tradition—a blessed thing to draw our family together. By carefully and lovingly preparing food, we can bring an element of peace and harmony to our families. As we grow in wisdom and grace, our prism will begin to shimmer with warmth that will be felt by all who enter our homes.

Special Problems

Some of us think that we are either too fat or too thin. We may be guilty, confused, or self-righteous about the way we eat or the way we prepare food for others. Food may be often in our thoughts and in our speech—and of course in our mouths! I don't want to discuss dieting here because there are many books that can help the dieter. Whether dieting or not, homemakers need to be concerned about food.

I have heard some women say, however, that they wish they would never have to eat again. They could save so much time, money, and energy if they did not have to eat. They simply rebel against the whole idea. This attitude can cause problems for the way we nurture our families. It can even cause problems in our relationship with God. When we rebel against our need for food, we actually rebel against God and the way that he has made us.

The opposite problem happens when someone enjoys food so much that they constantly use it for more than nurture. They take great delight in satisfying every desire of their appetite. When their body responds by becoming plump, they may feel rebellious about the kind of body they've been given. They probably wish they were the kind of person who could eat anything and everything without gaining weight. They fail to accept the person that God has made them to be.

Food can also become something of an idol for us. When we are depressed, we go hunting for "something good" to cheer us up. When we are nervous, we nibble. When we are angry, we may eat whatever is in sight. And when we are happy or hear good news, the first thing that comes to mind may be that we should celebrate with a fancy meal. In all these cases we are turning to food when we should be turning to the Lord. Anything that we put in God's place is an idol. When I first recognized that I sometimes made an idol out of food, I was astounded. Imagine the stupidity of it! What could food do for me that God couldn't? In fact, when I depended on food, I was postponing the victories God wanted over my depression, sadness, anxiety, and anger. And I was also taking the glory away from him by failing to give him thanks for good news. Though we often celebrate with food, our first thought upon hearing good news should not be—"Ah! An excuse to eat!"

The way to begin to overcome these problems is to repent and receive God's forgiveness. We can ask Jesus to fill all the empty places where we would have put food in the past. We can ask him to strengthen us in our fight against wishing we didn't need food or making it into an idol.

Another common problem happens when we try to satisfy our need for creativity at the expense of our family. For example, I really enjoy making different kinds of summer salads with cream cheese when the weather is hot. One summer I introduced these to my family. My husband was glad that I wanted to expand the family's acceptance of new foods but didn't like cream cheese in any salad. Therefore, I simply gave up making them for my family. If I had continued slipping them in once in a while, knowing my husband's objections, I would have been using food to further my own need to be creative. Instead, I saved cream cheese salads for my lunches.

We must also be careful not to compete with other women when we are extending them hospitality. If we are always trying to outdo each other, our pride won't let us really enjoy being together. And if something we make doesn't turn out quite as planned, our afternoon or evening will be ruined. What a waste! We should plan food to meet everyone's needs, including our own. If we are spending so much time making a fancy dish that we snap at our children for the slightest interruption, our priorities are probably out of order. If we overspend our budget in order to make a great dinner, we've chosen unwisely.

Recently, a friend of mine entertained a group of us who were trying to lose weight. She's an excellent cook and could have prepared any number of wonderful treats for a hot, summer evening. Instead she gave us watermelon in frosted bowls and cool drinks in frosted glasses. She had satisfied her desire to be creative by cooling the glasses and dishes, yet had shown concern for us by serving such a low-calorie treat.

Whatever the problem, it can be overcome by our willingness to die to ourselves in order to love and serve others. The right choices may not always be obvious. And we will need to rely on trial and error when making them. Since the needs of our families are often changing, we must be flexible enough to change with them. The important thing to remember is that we want to do all things out of love. If we do, our lamps will provide more "atmosphere" in our homes than the dinner candles at our most elegant or intimate dinners.

TEN

Your Husband and You

By now it should be evident that almost every prism we have picked up to clean and polish affects the other prisms of our lamps. We cannot separate a poor self-image from difficulties with guilt, for example, nor can we separate discouragement from anxiety or depression. We are complex individuals, the different colors of our personalities shimmering together, melting and taking on new hues. Our attempts at separation have been artificial but necessary in order to bring the light of God's truth to as many aspects of our lives as possible.

With this in mind, we can go on to discuss our relationships with our husbands. Who we are and what we bring to our marriages is very much tied up with the things we have already discussed. We cannot act as though these forces were not at work upon our personalities. At the same time it is also useful to examine the way we relate to our husbands in and of itself. In our marriages, for better or worse, our lamps are on a lampstand. There is no more exposed or vulnerable state than in marriage. No other person is in a position to know us better than our spouse, even though we may claim otherwise. Other folks do not have to live with us, an experience that can reveal many things that even the closest friends may never see.

Since you are reading this section, I will assume that you are either married or expect to be married in the future, and that you care about the quality of your life, both as an individual and as a marriage partner. You probably want to experience more peace in your life. You may think that the path to peace begins when your husband grows in the love of God and develops into a strong Christian man. Such a view implies that "If my husband were only holier, I could be, too."

Or perhaps your view is closer to the opposite end of the spectrum. You consider growth in holiness something that happens apart from your marriage. "He can do his thing, but I'm going to do mine."

Of course the proper perspective lies somewhere between the two. We need to accept the fact that God is working out our salvation in the midst of our marriage. Our sanctity isn't determined by our husband's level of holiness, nor is it being worked out in spite of who he is or apart from him. God has a particular plan for our marriage and for us individually in the context of that marriage.

Just like stones that are polished by rubbing against each other for a long time before their beauty begins to shine forth, so it is that a husband and wife polish one another in marriage. No doubt it can hurt to be rubbed smooth, but the result is a great work for the glory of God. And it is he who has to be the focus for our marriages (not that you need to convince your husband of that). Take your eyes off him and begin to put your eyes on the risen Savior, who will gently lead you in the way you must go. Trust Jesus not to let go of your husband. He's his Lord, too.

A Helpmate

Scripture says that God planned for us to be helpmates to our husbands. The New Testament tells us that we are to be submissive to them as to the Lord. Since I have written about this in my last book, *Do You Feel Alone in the Spirit?*, I will concentrate here on the subject of being a helpmate.

It's good to start with the knowledge that you are a strong and holy woman, imperfect, perhaps, but aware that you can do all things in him who strengthens you. If you approach your marriage from a position of personal strength, you will be in a much better place to support and encourage your husband. Too many women take the opposite approach. If you look at your husband as someone who should take care of you completely, fulfilling all your needs, you're guaranteed problems. No wonder so many marriages fail. That kind of expectation puts enormous pressure on the husband. Only God can take care of all our needs, and he has chosen to use the body of Christ to provide for us while we are on earth.

What does this mean concretely? My husband, for example, has little interest in sewing, cooking, or canning, other than to enjoy the finished product and encourage me to develop these skills. Yet, I need to discuss these things with others who share similar interests. And my husband encourages me to do this. It would be foolish to expect that he should learn everything he could about these subjects in order to fulfill my need to discuss and share ideas.

Every couple could probably draw up a catalog of unshared interests as well as ones they hold in common. I have always thought that if each developed their own interests, they would have more to talk about when they were together. Of course, it is also important to do things together that both can enjoy. And certainly both should learn to appreciate and respect the other's interests. It is reasonable to expect that both partners will encourage one another. We want to focus on how we as women can be helpmates, not on how our husbands may be failing us.

Our Husbands Are People Too

To develop a healthy attitude about what it means to be a helpmate, we need to step back from the routine of the day. We need to see our husband not primarily in his role as husband, father of our children, filler of needs, and inadequate at all three, but rather as a person, a man, your love for whom makes it a privilege to be his helpmate. There is a real, though sometimes subtle difference in those two ways of viewing our husbands. But be careful not to overspiritualize the relationship: "This is the man to whom God has covenanted me. I must love and serve him for the glory and honor of God." This may be true, but constant awareness of this fact may give our husbands the impression that we are living our married life as a duty. Sometimes during our marriages this is the only thing that will sustain us, but for the most part we need a more balanced approach. Our man is an individual, and we should see him as such, rather than just thinking of him in his role as husband, father, and provider. We don't want to take him for granted in any way.

Respect Him

Related to this, we need to respect and understand our men. As someone has said, "To understand you must stand under. When you stand under, you have to look up to—and that's the beginning of understanding."

To think that you understand your husband so well that you could not possibly respect him is to make a mockery of the gospel. Jesus came so that your husband could have life and have it abundantly. God loves and respects him enough to give him life, free will, and you for a wife. If you find it difficult to respect your husband, your brother in the Lord, pray for the grace to see him as Jesus does, to love him with Jesus' love and understanding.

Don't look at what a poor job your husband is doing at fulfilling his responsibilities or meeting your needs, if that is what you are doing, and look, instead, at how you might be a source of solace and strength to one scarred by his daily battle with life. Think about who your husband was before you married him. In most cases, the qualities that first attracted you to him are still there. Think of the scars you have both inflicted on each other and pray for God's mercy and his blessing on your lives together.

The Troublesome Tongue

Most of all, be careful how you talk about your husband. You might have had a fight and be feeling angry and hurt, but it is wrong to go around complaining about him, looking for ammunition or justification for your position. And if you think about it in a calmer moment, you know that you really want others to think well of your husband. Imagine, this is the man to whom you have committed your whole life. At a very basic level, it's a poor reflection upon your judgment if you paint your husband as a lousy person. It's unfortunate that so many women slip into bad-mouthing or belittling their husbands, Christian women who never think of speaking negatively about anyone else. It's important to be very careful about speech, especially about one's husband. The woman who tears down her husband in the eyes of others is certainly not being much of a helpmate.

If there are problems in your marriage that you need help with, look for a mature person who can counsel you. You may need to very carefully discuss some aspects of your married life that you would not normally talk about, but even in that situation, the focus should be on how you should respond in love and learn to cope with the difficulties. Counselling sessions should not become occasions for venting anger and frustration, for not only is this wrong, but it simply doesn't help. You may experience temporary relief from pressure, but such an experience encourages you to become bitter and puts the focus on your husband instead of on how you can be a godly woman in a difficult situation. I am not denying the need to deal with anger and hurt. I have spent time already discussing how to handle these difficult emotions. But I am saying that the temptation to express these emotions in a way that will prove more destructive than constructive is a strong one.

Be Peace-Bearers

In Old English there is a name for women that means peace-bearer. I have always liked to think of our role as a helpmate in terms of that word. The name implies strength and courage, for peace is a difficult load to carry in many situations. But by God's grace we can be strong enough to bring forth peace, to be healers in our families. For as God heals us, we know that it's not for our sake alone but for our families and for the whole body of Christ as well.

We do not bring forth peace by preaching the word of God, but by being the word of God—by letting the Father clean and polish us so we reflect his own love and concern for those he loves.

Remember to Communicate

One of the largest stumbling blocks that can come up in a marriage, and one that can be devastating if it goes unrecognized, has to do with mismatched expectations, something we discussed earlier, in the chapter on irritability. Both spouses expect to experience various things in their marriage, ranging from things as trivial as the choice of the supper meal to major life goals. And sometimes the trivial mismatched expectations are the ones that cause the most trouble.

For instance, your husband tells you, "Let's go out to eat Friday night."

Friday arrives and you have arranged for a baby-sitter and are dressed in one of your most elegant dresses, having spent most of the week picturing both of you at a very nice local restaurant, sharing a beautiful meal and intimate conversation. You are just in the mood for a quiet romantic evening.

Your husband comes in and asks why you're all dressed up. You respond by describing your expectations for the evening. "Oh, no," he explains laughingly, "we certainly can't afford that this month. Let's go to the golden arches and take in the new Clint Eastwood movie."

Only a woman who has experienced this type of scene (and I believe that will include most of us) will understand the explosive temper ignited, the hurt feelings, the struggle involved in having to change your mind at the last minute. Yet, neither husband nor wife intended harm to the other. Both wanted a nice evening together. Mismatched expectations like this can be cleared up in most marriages rather quickly by a little advance communication.

We can well imagine the following scenarios.

"I thought you would want to send them to parochial school."

"I never said that. I've always thought public schools were better."

"I thought we'd be going to my mom's for Thanksgiving. I already told her we'd be there around one."

"Call her back. I told my mom we'd be at her place by 1:30."

Problems like this can be avoided if you remember: to talk things over ahead of time; not to make definite plans with a third party on the basis of your assumptions; and to keep an open mind that may hope or even pray for certain outcomes but that doesn't count on them. Almost anything can go wrong with even the best-laid plans. Who can predict whether a child will become ill or whether some other household emergency will occur? Hope for the best, and know that you can count on Jesus to be there in the middle of whatever does happen.

Talk Things Over

It's important to talk things over with your husband regularly. Most people could stand improvement when it comes to communicating. I realize that giving general guidelines can be frustrating because marriages are made up of a wide variety of individuals, ranging from good listeners who never talk to those who talk constantly but rarely listen, and every combination and degree in between. Who you and your husband are will determine the aspects of speaking or listening that need to be emphasized. With this in mind, I would like to share some things I have learned about this area.

Communication obviously depends upon both of you, but you can make sure that you are holding up your side of the conversation. First, check your motives before you bring up a topic, especially if it has been an area of conflict in the past. Is it that your husband does not understand you or that he disagrees with you? Maybe you think that if you were only more eloquent or articulate he would have to agree with you. Not necessarily true. You need to believe that the man has ears.

And if you are going to him daily, or even weekly, with the same thought worded a different way, you have become a nag—a creative nag perhaps, but a nag nevertheless. If you have presented an area of concern to your husband once or twice and he still disagrees with you, let go of it and follow his lead. If it is an area of great concern, give it to the Lord, trusting him to bring good out of all things.

If it is an area of sin, there is no need for discussion. We are not supposed to sin. But be careful. I have known women for whom this truth has been twisted to mean, "It is sinful for my husband to be inconsiderate of my feelings in this matter, so I feel I am justified in doing it anyway." If your thought patterns border on this, you've slid onto dangerous ground. Seek the Lord and ask him to give you a pure heart and a humble spirit. Be quick to repent of a proud spirit that would engage in a power struggle in the name of righteousness, and be quick to accept forgiveness. And remember to laugh at yourself. It helps to recall what funny creatures we sometimes are.

We're on the Same Side

Power struggles between husband and wife can take many forms. Sometimes they occur in the area of chores or recreation. About twice a year my husband and I discuss recreational needs. At home with five children, I am apt to desire recreation outside the home with other people. My husband, a busy attorney and college professor, is more likely to want a quiet evening at home. We have had to work on ways to meet both of our needs, by understanding one another, and by letting one another know honestly how we are feeling. We must be willing to sacrifice for the other and to remind each other if we become upset, "Hey, wait a minute! We're on the same side."

That's probably one of the most useful phrases in my marriage. It reminds us that we want to provide mutual care and support, that we're not looking for ways to convince the other to start taking better care of our needs. We are partners who are different and who must expect that we will need to work things out occasionally. But what a difference it makes to see that first of all we are on the same side.

It is bound to happen that seasons for self-sacrifice and extra care will vary in your marriage. Sometimes your need might be legitimately great, but you will see that your husband's need may be greater. In the desire to be a good helpmate, you will make the extra effort to fight resentment and defer gratification of your own needs for the sake of your husband's. Be careful not to fall into the suffering martyr complex, however, which makes you too strong to accept offers of care and concern. You need to be cared for, too. And fight the temptation to protect your husband from bad news. He may not need to hear everything the minute he walks in the door. Timing, after all, is important. But if you have great concerns, he will need to hear about them before too long.

Discussing Your Relationship

If you need to discuss your relationship itself with your husband, take great care in the language you use. A helpmate seeks the good of the other and will try to bring out the best in the other. You can't accomplish this by taking the offensive. Discussions on the quality of your relationship or on some aspect of your husband's behavior that you dislike usually either begin or quickly degenerate into accusations. If you hear yourself starting your sentences with "you," or especially "you're not," then you have probably crossed over from discussion into accusation.

"But I'm talking about an awful habit he has!" you may cry out. "How can I get him to change if I don't talk about it?"

What is really at issue here may not be your husband's habit, per se, but its effect on you or the rest of the family. If it's a small thing, you could forbear out of love, ask him why he does it a particular way, or simply tell him that it disturbs you and ask him if he would stop. This way you are letting your husband know of your concerns and your needs rather than discussing his failings. In all matters, great or small, your husband may be quite willing to change if he knows why his actions are upsetting others. You can discuss your emotions or observations of the children and its connection, perhaps, with a certain habit of your husband's. If you start the discussion by castigating him, you have immediately put him on the defensive and created another power struggle.

Instead of, "Your habit of leaving dirty ashtrays around all the time drives me up the wall!" try, "Honey, I don't mind emptying ashtrays and picking up from late-night snacks, but I can't always keep ahead of the baby. He's able to pull himself up now, and this week I found him eating cigarette butts a couple of times. Could you try to put the ashtrays up higher or empty them yourself when you're through?" That way you've identified what bothers you most about your husband's habit, but you've done it in a straightforward and loving way.

Don't try to legitimize something that is only a matter of personal taste. Remember to check your motives. We can pick the most trivial subjects as the field for the most major battles. The more trivial the cause of your emotional response, the more you should guard against it sparking a power struggle. It helps to go to the Lord and meditate on what it means to be a helpmate, a good wife, and a holy woman of God.

Conflicts over daily household issues are inevitable for another reason as well. You entered your marriage with a set of experiences gained from years of living with your parents, and your husband entered into it with a whole different set. Things which you have taken for granted may never have entered your husband's consciousness, and the reverse is probably also true. You may find yourself outraged with your husband, mentally convicting him of boorishness, when he is innocently living life the way he was brought up. It is important to remember that the fact that you lived daily life differently before your marriage does not mean that one way was right and another wrong, or even that one was better than another. Learn from your past experiences within your respective families, but realize that God is doing a new thing with your new family. Conflicts are bound to occur, but in all things seek God's will. When you think about it, you'll realize that in many areas it does not really matter how you do something. If it doesn't matter, why make it a bone of contention? In all things try to be a helpmate. In all circumstances try to remember that you and your husband are on the same side.

ELEVEN

Providing a Good Life in the Home

It's clear in the preceding chapters that the cleaner and more polished our prisms become, the more clearly we will reflect God's love in the environment in which he has placed us. We will become greater channels of his grace to others. Most of us have a great deal to do with creating and maintaining the physical environment in which we are placed, whether within our homes, or, to a lesser extent, on our jobs.

Whether we rejoice and revel in our responsibility to care for our homes or only scrape by with the bare minimum, we cannot escape the fact that unless we do something, things will simply fall apart. I have occasionally met women who are really pleased, confident, and at peace with their homes and their daily routines. More often I've known of women who are frustrated and confused, feeling helpless to even begin to create order or beauty out of the chaos. And, of course, many of us are somewhere in between.

Mythical Standards

Magazines and books that offer decorating tips seem to presume that women have a great deal of time and money to create a home that is a worthwhile place to live, one that expresses the "true you." Even if you only look through magazines at the doctor's office, this philosophy can affect you. The homes in the background of most television commercials would require at least one full-time servant to maintain them and would allow for no more than two *very* careful and well-trained children to inhabit them. Most of us must battle the sense of failure that stems from the simple fact that we cannot maintain our homes according to this mythical standard of perfection.

Just what should our standards be? All of us probably cherish an ideal of what we want our homes to look like. And that ideal will differ from woman to woman. Some care little about order but concentrate instead on the flow of life which takes place within the home. Some insist on strict standards of order and cleanliness, failing to tolerate the slightest hint of dust or disorder. Some women who once thought they knew what their homes should be have become overwhelmed by the task and have given up, hoping to get through each day the best they can.

Having Christian Goals

All of this points out two main truths about our role as homemaker. First, caring for the home is almost exclusively our responsibility. Second, the way we care for them will vary from woman to woman, depending on the peculiar array of circumstances surrounding our lives. Even so, as Christian women, we can work toward certain goals that will help create a good environment in our homes, no matter our circumstances.

Just as we should reflect the work and glory of God, so should our homes. Certain characteristics or qualities of God—truth, unity, beauty, and order—lend themselves most fully to an understanding of how to create, prepare, and maintain the physical environment of the home. These may strike you as too ethereal for your situation. What does truth or beauty have to do with dirty laundry, mismatched socks, empty Coke bottles, or messy diapers? Well, bear with me. I live in the real world, too. I have no maid or housekeeper, but I do have five children, and I spend a good deal of time at this typewriter. It is possible to look at such an abstract goal and form specific plans that will help us attain it. As always, the first step is prayer. Go before the Father humbly to ask for his wisdom, fully confident that he will grant it. Remember, your confidence is in him, not yourself or your circumstances. Make a list of areas that should concern you as you consider what it means to provide a good life in the home. These would include such things as decorating skills, knowledge about furniture, sewing, cooking, recreation and celebration ideas, cleanliness skills, and the ability to put order into life. As a good servant in the Lord's kingdom, you can use these skills to serve him and his people.

Once you have listed these, consider whether you are holding on to any attitude that might prevent you from taking on God's mind in any of these areas. Such attitudes include the fear of failure, discouragement, a poor self-image, depression, avarice, resentment that you haven't time or money to do just what you would like, envy or covetousness, and a competitive spirit. Go before the Lord with a teachable heart, asking him to reveal to you anything that may be preventing you from doing his will. If he points out obstacles, repent and be forgiven with a glad and grateful heart. Even if you don't spot any of these attitudes in yourself, guard against them. Don't let them creep in later as you view and review the care of your home.

Once you've come this far, take your list of concerns in the home and note your strengths and weaknesses regarding each. Acknowledge any gifts you may have artistically, in regard to sewing, cooking, physical endurance, arts and crafts, creativity, and so on. Don't be afraid to admit your weaknesses. Once you've done so, you can realistically proceed to build on your strengths, learning to overcome or to live creatively with your weaknesses. For instance, you may know that you are an excellent seamstress but lack the time or talent to can fruits or vegetables. You might strike a bargain with a friend who cans but has difficulty threading a needle. You'll sew for her if she'll can for you or you'll teach her to sew and she'll show you how to can.

If we approach the task of assessing our strengths and weaknesses humbly, in the knowledge that God comes first and that our life is a gift from him, we won't become conceited about our talents nor dejected about our weaknesses. God is the giver of every gift. And, in areas where we lack expertise, he can help us to overcome what may just be ignorance.

For instance, I may want to purchase a particular style of furniture for my living room, but may hesitate because I know very little about wearable fabrics and mistrust my sense of color coordination. That ignorance can be remedied by a trip to the library for some good books, or by a simple eight-week course at the local "Y." Even when money is a real problem, it does not hurt to be educated so that we can make good choices of second-hand furniture.

A Vision of Truth

What does this have to do with truth, unity, order, and beauty? To reflect truth, our homes must not project an "image" that would lead us into debt. We should do our best to decorate our homes in a way that is true to the needs of our families. If our natural inclination is to do otherwise, we should set it aside for the Lord's sake, as well as the sake of our families. If we choose the kind of furniture that children can't use without being constantly admonished, then we have erred in our choice. Light-colored, silk-covered couches don't belong in the home of preschoolers. Also, glass tabletops, lamps, and decorations should be used sparingly and in protected spots if our homes are full of children. To assume that young children will be as careful as these objects require is simply unrealistic.

The Quality of Unity and Simplicity

Most definitions of unity mention the word "simplicity." Though it's difficult to find a definition of unity or simplicity that fits every style of home, suffice it to say that our homes should neither be too ornate nor too "fussy." If we aren't careful our homes can become idols to us. Though we should strive to be good stewards and good servants, God comes first, and the needs of our families second. Something can always be done to fix up a home, but at some point we've got to stop and be at peace for a time. Of course, I'm not talking about normal maintenance needs. We can be so full of ideas that we become almost frantically obsessed with them and frustrated if progress is slow or our husbands are unwilling to comply. Simplicity and unity would caution us to be careful in determining what *needs* to be done. Above all, we should earnestly desire God's wisdom in making these choices.

A Vision of Order

Most of us have experienced the frustration that comes from not knowing where to find the string, the tape, the pencils, or the scissors. Of course, this may not be entirely our fault. Even grown men and women have been known not to return tape to its rightful home. But our responsibility is to see that everything does have a proper place and does not spend its brief life roaming all over the house. Anyone who has lived through the frantic pace of getting her children off to school and her husband to work on time, and perhaps even getting ready for work herself, can appreciate the value of good order in the home.

How do you know if your home is well-ordered? A good guideline or test is to picture yourself confined to bed, unable to show anyone around, but needing to explain to someone how to run your house during your month of confinement. Do you know where the vacuum cleaner, cleaning supplies, and rags are kept? Can you say with certainty where the groceries should all be stored? Is there an order to the linen or must one rummage through it all every time a sheet needs changing? What method do you use for sorting laundry and getting it back in the proper drawers? Do the keys, notebooks, pocketbooks, newspapers, magazines, school papers, calendars, phone numbers, and pens have a home, or are they always turning up somewhere new? How do you handle your correspondence? What are the ten most frequently sought after items that your family has difficulty locating? Answering these questions will go a long way toward helping you to place your home in good order. If you do have designated places for certain items that never seem to be there, you should think of a more workable place.

A Vision of Beauty

Finally, our homes should reflect the beauty of God's kingdom. Now in his mansion there are many rooms, and I am sure that they do not all look alike. But surely they do not jar the eye with mismatched colors or unrelieved plainness. Just as my great aunt's drawing room was brightened by the presence of a prism lamp, our rooms should have little touches that reflect the beauty that God has created. Something need not be expensive to be beautiful. Dried flowers, fresh cut flowers from our gardens, banners, and wall hangings can be relatively inexpensive. If not skilled in these arts yourself, perhaps a friend could make something you would like if you supplied the materials.

One of my friend's homes has beautiful pictures adorning its walls. At first glance you would think she had done this at great expense. But my friend had simply cut pictures she liked from magazines or cards and framed them inexpensively. The overall effect is simply lovely.

Another friend has developed a green thumb and her home is also a place of beauty. She has patiently started her plants from tiny cuts off other plants, and the pots that she uses are mainly refurbished white elephants. So, again, with very little expense, a beautiful effect has been created, which gives life and color to a home.

Yet another woman I know has inherited a set of Hummel figurines which grace the shelves of many of the rooms in her home. She has wisely and lovingly placed these out of the reach of small visitor's hands but not out of range of their eyes.

Whatever our gifts or preference in style, let us not be ashamed for our homes to reflect God's beauty, just as we should not be ashamed of our personal appearance. At the same time, if money, time, or some other factor has prevented us from decorating our homes as we would like, let us not be ashamed of that either. When I was newly married my home didn't have proper curtains. I did the best I could to arrange coverings for them, but I had to tell myself that if the King of Kings were to visit my home, he would know that I had done the best I could according to my circumstances, that what I had done was done in love. Knowing that, I didn't have to feel ashamed or make excuses.

Some days, if you were to walk into my home, you would be hard-pressed to discover the underlying order as my children and I move through the tasks of our day. But I am working with a plan and a schedule, and by the end of the day, except on rare occasions, the house is neat and clean. When company drops by unexpectedly in the middle of the day, however, I have to fight the temptation to make excuses for myself, battling the mythical standard of perfection that the world puts forth. We must strive to keep uppermost in our minds that we are serving in God's mansion for his honor and glory.

Once you have thought these things through, you ought to talk over your concerns with your husband. If possible, you should pray together for God's direction for your home and family life. Try to determine, for example, if God has called you to make hospitality a major priority. Has he called you to evangelism, and, if so, to any group in particular? Are you mainly concerned with opening your home to teenagers, to preschoolers, or to the aged? Or do you use your home mainly as a haven and place of relaxation and peace for the family, because your time and energy are mainly required elsewhere? Discovering God's purpose for your home will help you make the right choices regarding furniture, decorations, and accessories, including such things as ping-pong and picnic tables. It will help you to know how much time and energy to spend on pursuits such as sewing, cooking, and arts and crafts.

It would be foolish for most women to try to become involved in sewing, canning, macrame projects, and tutoring while holding a full-time job outside the home. This kind of involvement may even prove too difficult for a woman who spends all her time within the home. Even though you enjoy a certain hobby or interest, you may need to give it up for a season in order to serve those around you.

If you cannot pray with your husband about these things, you can pray about them yourself. Ask the Lord to give you and your husband wisdom and to help you to be open to change should your husband see the need for it. Then talk your ideas over with your husband. Since he is the head of the house, any major changes should be approved by him.

A friend of mine was leading a very busy life, helping her husband with his business part time, caring for her home and children, canning, and sewing almost all of her children's clothes. She had planned to have a full garden in the summer when it occurred to her to talk to her husband first about her plans. He realized that her time was already being put to better use. A garden would only complicate matters. With her husband's guidance, she was able to avoid a situation that could have spoiled the summer for her and possibly for her family as well. In addition, he was able to help her put more reasonable limits on the amount and type of food that she canned, in order to free her schedule still more.

Another woman I know was involved in so many charitable works outside the home that everyone thought she was a wonder-worker. But her husband told her to drop out of all but one activity for at least six months while she established more order in the home—until he could be sure to have clean clothes and meals that were substantial. He needed to know that she had her priorities straight and was putting the needs of the family first. Though she experienced a great deal of pain in following her husband's advice, this woman gradually realized the wisdom of her husband's request. When her house was finally in order again, and she was free to return to her charitable activities, she did so more selectively, taking care not to get involved in more than she could manage.

For some of you, who must work full time outside the home, making quick meals and cutting corners are a necessary part of life. You can minimize the frustrations if your family cooperates with cleaning and maintaining order, and if you can follow a fairly rigorous schedule; but you should not expect yourself to accomplish as much as if you were home all day.

Obviously time is an important factor to consider when making decisions about the home environment. Another important factor is money. You can have all the knowledge necessary to make a good purchase of carpeting, paintings, or furniture, but if you haven't got the money, there's not much you can do about it. In general, though, it usually pays to get the best quality you can possibly afford in furniture—even if you have to wait awhile or must sacrifice something else in your budget. Quality will determine how long furniture will last. Even so, some of you are not in a position to consider buying new furniture. If that's the case, try to get a good deal on used furniture when you need it. Be patient and pray for the furniture God wants you to have. I know of some families with beautifully furnished homes who have spent less than $500 total, due to the generosity of family and friends and the graciousness of God.

Celebration

A good life in the home involves time for celebration and recreation. We should give some thought to the way that we celebrate holidays and special family days. We can share ideas with friends or do a little reading to give us some fresh ideas. We need not take a week of preparation to make an event special, but simple ideas that match the needs of our family can mean much.

For instance, I know of families with preschoolers who have a birthday cake for Jesus on Christmas. To young children a cake means "birthday" and therefore most effectively conveys the meaning of the day. Another family I know routinely gives special presents on birthdays, like one family providing free babysitting for a month for the young couple across the street, a son washing windows for his mother, or a mother offering to clean her son's room.

As wives and mothers we know the special things that might touch our families' hearts. We can ask God for the creativity to think of these. They need not be original ideas but need only be performed out of love.

Four Spiritual Tools

In all the areas where we have concern for our homes four spiritual tools will help us above all others—faithfulness, flexibility, humility, and love. We should make it our business to actively seek these things.

We know that our lives will require faithfulness, for our work is always before us, demanding great energy, effort, and endurance. And the relationships within the family will always need our gentle care and concern. May God make us as faithful to our family as he is to his. To give us hope as we endure, let us keep in mind that there are seasons in our lives, some more enjoyable than others, but all to be used by God for our strengthening and his glory. Let us pray, too, for the grace to thoroughly enjoy the pleasant seasons, to overcome tribulation in the difficult seasons, and to rejoice and be thankful for whatever God brings with each.

We must be flexible. A friend of mine with five children under the age of seven has a sign in her kitchen: "God came to change all my plans." We can have a marvelous schedule that will nevertheless need changing ten times before the morning is over. We should expect that emergencies and interruptions will form a regular part of life. We can meet every situation with courage, however, if we keep in mind that we are not adrift and alone in our homes. God is there to guide and strengthen us in every circumstance.

What about humility? Should a woman be proud of her home? Certainly we should experience the good feeling of accomplishment and confidence that accompanies a job well-done. Our temptation will be to think of our lives in terms of "my house, my family, my day, and my time." Let us pray for the humility to know instead that it is God's home, God's families, God's day, and God's time. We can rejoice that the Lord is working in our lives, enabling us to be good wives and mothers. But we must remember that in all things we live to reflect the light of the Lord. We are not ourselves the source of light.

"Love covers a multitude of sins." That has to be one of the most comforting passages of scripture. We may not be Christian Wonder Women, and we will certainly meet frustration and disappointment in ourselves, our efforts, and our families. We will make mistakes and will even sin, needing to repent and seek reconciliation. But love covers a multitude of sins. If, despite all our rough edges, we consistently put the best interests of our families first, they will know of our love and flourish. Let us pray for God's mercy and love to be poured out daily upon each member of our family, including ourselves. Let us strive to be the strong and holy women God has called us to be. And "Let our hope keep us joyful." Let us seek God's grace to believe that his love and mercy will make up for what is lacking in us.

We are to do the best we can to create and maintain the environment God wants in our homes, to reflect his glory. But, ultimately, it is God's family. We cannot be the Holy Spirit to our families. Only God can change hearts. So let us serve out of love for God, with our hope firmly established in him. Let us yield to him so that we may become his women. And then let us be content.

Afterword

Having examined our prism lamps for dust and dirt, we should realize that the cleaning and restoration that they need can't be provided simply by reading a book. However, we now have the great advantage of knowing the work that needs to be done and knowing which tools can accomplish the job.

It's important that we allow the work of cleaning and maintaining our lamps to be accomplished in the right climate, and that climate is hope. None of us will become brightly cleaned and polished in a day. It will hurt to have the dirt dug out of cracks and crannies, to have new wires replace the old, to have the rust removed and the metal restored. But we needn't simply focus on the work at hand. We need to dwell lovingly and trustingly on the One who will be restoring us. It is he who is merciful, patient, and tender-hearted, having created us in his own image. His Spirit works in all our hidden places to help us to reflect the glory of our Creator.

Let our hope keep us joyful, remembering that even in the midst of our weakness God can be glorified. Although change may come slowly and we stumble and fall many times, we shall move forward, becoming holier and stronger women. As we give up our own ways for God's, we shall be blessed many times over. Let us not fear to die to ourselves. Such death brings new life. Knowing that, let us welcome it, embracing it out of love for Jesus, who died for us.

As we overcome our personal problems and work at making love a reality in our lives, we will begin to experience an inner peace and joy that no one can take from us. For we will have the assurance that we are pleasing our Beloved. He knows our frailty and weaknesses and tells us not to fear them. He will replace them with his righteousness and his strength.

Our lives will endure many difficult seasons, but as Christians we are not left to walk the path alone. Jesus himself is the way to his Father's house. Let us rejoice and be glad. Let us throw off the fetters that bind us, in order to walk in his glorious kingdom. Let us dare to become strong and holy women, so that God's glory may blaze the brighter throughout the world.

Recent Lakeland paperbacks

DISCIPLE

Juan Carlos Ortiz

Disciple tells of a spiritual revolution which transformed a Christian congregation in Buenos Aires, based on a new awareness of the total Lordship of Christ in the life of the believer. Sharing his discoveries about the meaning of discipleship, Juan Carlos Ortiz writes with shrewdness and humour. Gently questioning many of our most cherished traditions and habits of worship he forces us to re-examine them in the light or revealed Scripture and exposes the shallowness of our claims to be followers of Jesus.

This is a challenging, at times controversial book. You may disagree with it, but you cannot ignore it.

CRY OF THE HUMAN HEART

Juan Carlos Ortiz

A further challenge to a new and power-filled way of life.

Juan Carlos Ortiz believes that many Christians are frustrated, and disappointed with themselves because they cannot fulfil that deepest cry of their hearts – to please God. This book is about the way out of this dilemma.

Recent Lakeland paperbacks

UNDER GOD'S WORD

Jim Packer

Is the Bible all true? And is it important that it should be? Jim Packer, the bestselling author of KNOWING GOD, takes a decisive stand on these questions. But he goes beyond the issue of inerrancy to the more important one of authority – what is the point of winning the battle for the Bible if in the process we lose our understanding of its role? The Bible is central to both personal and public worship. To recover truly biblical faith and practice we need to restore the Bible to its rightful place in the lives of present-day Christians and churches.

Writing with a deep pastoral concern Jim Packer brings us back to devotion and worship as the key to understanding God's word and appropriating it for ourselves. UNDER GOD'S WORD is a challenging reminder that it is nothing less than our souls which are at stake in this debate.

WHY I BELIEVE

D. James Kennedy

Do you know what Christians believe, and why they believe it? Can you defend your belief against the critics all around you?

Dr D. James Kennedy, the world renowned founder of Evangelism Explosion International, was so angry when he heard a militant atheist make mincemeat out of the Christian callers-in to a radio talk show he had to do something. From his lifetime of study he has brought together a compellingly powerful declaration of what Christians believe and why ... intelligent, informed responses to frequently heard objections to the Christian faith.

Intensely penetrating and personal, this book is a statement you will want to make your own.

THE GOLDEN COW
Materialism in the Twentieth-century Church
John White

Is it possible that the church today has begun worshipping the golden cow of materialism and success? John White begins to answer this question by considering the property-centred outlook of many churches whose evangelistic and church-building endeavours are governed more by mass psychology than by prayerful planning. Then he examines the fund-raising techniques of Christian organizations. Turning to Christian businesses, he asks whether they have become desensitized to what is sacred. Finally, the author moves into the frequently statistic-ridden realm of evangelism. In this prophetic book John White asks us to consider whether we, too, are worshipping the golden cow.

"I believe this book is destined to be one of the most upsetting, thoughtprovoking, and powerful books of this decade." – *George Verwer*